religion

a beginner's guide

religion

a beginner's guide

martin forward

ONEWORLD

OXFORD

For Mary Ann

religion: a beginner's guide

Oneworld Publications
(Sales and Editorial)
185 Banbury Road
Oxford OX2 7AR
England
http://www.oneworld-publications.com

© Martin Forward 2001

ISBN 1–85168–258–9

Cover design: Bridgewater Book Company
Typeset by Saxon Graphics Ltd, Derby
Printed and bound in Great Britain by Creative Print and Design

Cover photographs: (second left) Jain *tirthankara* (ford crosser)
or *jina* (victor), Osian, Rajasthan. Photograph, Nancy M. Martin,
from *Ethics in the World Religions*, Oxford, Oneworld.
(right) Tenzin Gyatso, the fourteenth Dalai Lama.
Photograph courtesy of John Strong, from
A Concise Encyclopedia of Buddhism, Oxford, Oneworld.

contents

acknowledgements

I am extremely grateful to Juliet Mabey for asking me to write this book, and to her colleagues at Oneworld for bringing it to birth. I was privileged to give the Sir David James Lecture for 1998 at the University of Wales, Bangor, under the title 'Gods, Guides and Gurus: Theological Reflections on Travels with my Aunt'. I was also honoured to give the Teape Seminars in Cambridge University's Faculty of Divinity in January and February 1999, on the theme of 'The Divine in Human Form in India'. Some of the material from the lecture and seminars has found its way into this book.

I am indebted to lots of people for the facts and interpretation that are offered herein. Many authors and friends have tutored me in the things of religion. I apologise for often failing to mention them or even remember their precise influence. Like all teachers, I am very obliged to my students, who have listened to and often improved ideas like those included herein. I am especially grateful to Jonathan Dean.

In particular, I would like to acknowledge the debt I owe to three people. The first is to Professor David Craig. When he was Executive Producer for Religion in the BBC's World Service, we travelled together in South Asia, Africa and America to make radio programmes. Those experiences and David's acute observations taught me much about the variegated phenomenon of religion. I am much obliged to him. I am also thankful to two Methodist scholars of religion (the Methodist Church is my own spiritual home). The first is Geoffrey Parrinder. His pioneering work in Comparative Religion opened up to his successors the possibility that it makes sense to compare the religions of the world, and that that comparison should be made sympathetically, not in a polemical attempt to contrast the best in one's own religion with the worst in another's. I have made use of Professor Parrinder's creative work in this book, and am obliged to him. Even if sometimes I have provided different answers, he raised many of the important questions a long time ago.

The second Methodist scholar to whom I am indebted is Eric Lott. His careful and illuminating works have been unwisely under-appreciated by the wider academic world. His commitment to India and its religions, to liturgy, to ecology and to his friends has been inspirational to me and to many others. I offer this book to him and to his wife Christine, my very dear friends: a small token of thanks, admiration and love.

I would like to extend this dedication to two other people: to my wife Udho; and to my daughter Naomi, in the hope that she will find religion to be the source of fascination, discovery, excitement, comfort, hope and challenge that it has proved for me.

introduction

It is intriguing to be asked to write a beginner's guide to religion. In one sense, all humans are novices in this area, since religion provides an ocean of knowledge in which all may paddle but only a few wade further. Even saints and other holy people (perhaps especially these) acknowledge their limited comprehension in the face of the mysteries embodied and intuited by faith-structures.

Yet in another sense the title of this book would make no sense to many people born outside the Western world. They do not come to religion as beginners but as life-long participants. Religion is no more a choice for or a novelty to them than is their family. For them, religion is a relevant, enduring and universal fact of the human condition. From earliest times, there are signs that people believed in an afterlife or, at least, were lost in wonderment at the enigma of death. A number of factors have separated humans from other species: their capacity to communicate by language and thus co-operate with each other in sophisticated ways being chief amongst them. No doubt, by the medium of such things as campfire stories, early people reflected on: the meaning of dreams; the relation of the sky and the earth; the rhythms of life in the world around them and, for women, in their own bodies. All this became the stuff of mystery and wonder about the meaning of things. From very early times, humans became involved in the web of ritual, culture, and other factors that we call religion, which has provided a structure within which mystery can be grasped, enacted and lived out. So religion became and remains for most people a fact of life that has sustained them from cradle to grave. (Even so, there have been notable but rare exceptions, even in ancient times.)

This is not the case in certain parts of the world today; mainly in the West and in large urban centres elsewhere. The assumption that a person should choose to belong to a religion or not is by and large a relatively modern Western phenomenon. Nowadays, many such people are cut off from their religious roots, and know very little about their ancestral faith, usually but not always Christianity. They hardly ever enter its places of worship, read its sacred texts, follow its rites and rituals. When they ponder religion, they really are beginners. Many of them rather despise it as fit only for old people contemplating their mortality and others who search foolishly after an unreal security. Such disdainful people often have little but prejudice by which to make their judgement; certainly not much factual or deep experiential knowledge. (The USA provides a rare and intriguing exception, since one recent survey records that fifty-two per cent of its population still attend church.)

Secularism in the West, which often influences or even seems to demand such negative verdicts, can be a totalitarian phenomenon. Secularism comes from a word meaning 'this age'. It is often only interested in ephemeral, palpable, sensory things and is deeply suspicious of claims that there may be other intuitive and eternal modes of knowing and being. It frequently assumes that it is the norm from which all other beliefs, including those of the great world faiths, differ eccentrically. The tendency of this mode of knowledge has been to reduce the world to an object of technological research, stripping it bare of mystery. So the sacred canopy under which humankind for most of its history has sheltered, developed and matured has, for large numbers of people in the West, blown away, leaving them alone, commanders of their own destiny. People of other cultures, and an increasing number of Westerners too, have strongly criticised this point of view, yet there are points in its favour. Indeed, it is to the Western Enlightenment tradition of critical scholarship, the mother of secularism but the child of religion, that in certain respects I am indebted for the shaping of my own life and beliefs. Its emphasis upon reason, its suspicion of superstition, and its willingness to question authority: these are things many religious people dislike, but which, even if they are sometimes overstated by the uncomprehendingly irreligious, have proved profoundly beneficial to humankind. Other legacies of the Enlightenment have brought the planet to the brink of extinction. We should treat this tradition to friendly and respectful criticism, just as secularists would do well to approach religion in the same spirit.

I am primarily a scholar of the relatively new discipline of religious studies. Although such intellectuals are often practising members of a particular religion (I myself am a Methodist minister), they attempt to understand and appreciate other ways of responding to mystery. That is the perspective from where I stand. I am particularly grateful to and deeply influenced by the Christian tradition within which I have been nurtured and tutored. It has offered me a profound and challenging religious vision of and route through my life. Many secular readers are suspicious and dismissive of this perspective. Yet it shaped the Enlightenment movement, which in turn has also deeply and sometimes eccentrically moulded it.

Books communicate through words. So do human beings, but there are other powerful ways of communicating. Gesture, silence, intuitive thought and action: these are sometimes more powerful than words. Human beings create language as a vehicle for understanding in this mundane existence. Even so, it is sometimes a poor substitute for a hug or some other sign.

If language is not always adequate within this sensory world, how much more so when it attempts to convey an ultimate reality beyond human construction. When we come to look at sacred writings in chapter 3, we shall see a particular illustration of the power of words, yet we must also recognise their shortcomings. Despite the assumptions or assertions of scriptural literalists, in practice they do not deal with holy writ as a body of timeless truths. They interpret it, often from a narrow and limited perspective that they confuse with the eternal will of God. Also, they supplement it with other means by which they can locate Transcendent presence: for example, with holy places and holy people.

Our thoughts and images are caught up in the web of language. Religious language creates myths: for example, the myths of polytheism and monotheism that we shall discuss in chapter 2. The word myth does not mean that these notions are untrue. Rather, it reminds us that they point to a truth or truths beyond the power of the written word to convey. Language should not be used to trap the divine but rather to illuminate it, to 'see' it and be seen by it; some Indian religious traditions particularly emphasise this insight. So as we turn to this book's intention, I should emphasise its desire to 'see' ultimate reality with the inner eye of faith. Our task is to discern the eternal by using words, a human construct, not to fall into the folly of thinking that we can explain or even explain away ultimate reality by prosaic pedantry.

there's more to life than meets the eye

Lots of people want instant access to spiritual truths that mostly take a lifetime to gain and ponder. In chapter 4, we shall encounter Rabbi Hillel, a famous first century BCE teacher in Israel, responding to a man who was prepared to give a few seconds of his life to hear about the heart of religion. When my students want a quick fix on religion, part of me wants to send them away with a flea in their ear (the quite understandable response of Hillel's great contemporary, Rabbi Shammai, to the man who then got slightly more out of Hillel). Usually, the Hillel-bit of me wins out, and when they ask what is the core of religion, I tell them, 'There's more to life than meets the eye.'

Despite my particular faith stance, this book is certainly not a history, still less a zealous endorsement, of the Christian religion. Nor is it an introduction to the many and varied religions of the world. Many such introductions are available, written from fascinatingly different points of view. Two of the best of these are recorded in the bibliography: by Huston Smith (1991) and Ninian Smart (1998). Rather, this book is an exploration, even celebration, of the diversity as well as the touching points of religion. We shall look for underlying connections between variant expressions of faith, but differences will not be overlooked or played down.

My intention is to write a beginner's guide to religion that will interest people in this enduring phenomenon rather more than in the passing fancies of this age, which are the concern of secular values. I trust it will prove useful to them and to all who want to understand something of humankind's spiritual quest.

I write with an enthusiast's zeal for his subject. I spent my childhood in different parts of the world, observing much of the faith of Confucianists, Buddhists, Muslims and Jews before I ever heard of the Methodist form of Christianity that is now my home. I was entranced with the wonder of a child, which so many adults foolishly mistake for gullibility, by humankind's divergent expressions of the spiritual quest. I hope that some who read this book will be captivated by and drawn into the mystery of faith.

Chapter 1 asks 'What is religion?'. Chapter 2, 'Is anyone or something there?', explores the deep-rooted notion in the human heart, mind and spirit that there is more to life than meets the eye. What is that more? How have humans described it? Is it totally other than and different from humans, or somehow, even if elusively, located within this world of the senses? Chapter 3, 'How the Transcendent sees us and we see the Transcendent', illustrates how people throughout the centuries have attempted to respond to that dimension to life that is, in some ways, more than meets the eyes. So it discusses what has come to be termed 'spirituality' by many in the West. Chapter 4 is entitled 'The Good Life'. It describes what religions demand of their adherents in terms of an orientation towards the world. Is this life an end in itself, or simply one stage of a journey? What should our attitude be to the world of the senses that we inhabit here and now? What should we do in this life, and why? How far should our goodwill extend? Chapter 5, 'Religion in the New Millennium', looks at the challenges facing religion in the contemporary world, and hazards a few guesses about its future importance.

This is not a comprehensive survey of the phenomenon of religion. Neither space nor my own competence permit such an attempt. I have tended to concentrate on religions of West and South Asia. It seems best not to venture too far into areas that would unnecessarily expose my ignorance! As it is, I have no doubt made some errors of fact and even more of insight, for which I ask pardon. Religion is one of the humane (not just human) sciences; how hard it is to understand and appreciate the immense variety of human ways of being faithful, yet how important to try to do so.

To express my intentions clearly and sharply: this book candidly emphasises my personal vision and interpretation of the central importance of religion. I attach particular significance to the conviction that religion points to a phenomenon beyond itself and this mundane existence: to what theists would call God; though Buddhists and others would use other terminology. I have often used a term like *Transcendent reality* in the text below. Although this is cumbersome, it has the merit of reminding the reader that this is not a book about my own confessional stance. It is by no means the case that even all religious people in the modern world believe in the phenomenon known (amongst other terms) as God or Transcendence, as we shall see. I would certainly not call these sceptics irreligious, but I would contend that they miss religion's most important dimension and its greatest and most wondrous mystery. I also recognise that even for some deeply spiritual people, the word Transcendence seems inappropriate. Many indigenous people or 'first people', for example, have a holistic view of living and dying that can seem to preclude an outside dimension of reality that erupts into ordinary and mundane existence. Even so, we shall see that such people often have a strong belief in spirit or spirits, who introduce a mystical but very real dimension to existence. If 'Transcendence' is not a perfect word, it will have to suffice in this book as connoting a reality that is greater than the five senses describe and descry, and which often evokes a sense of awe and wonder in humans.

Some contemporary scholars of the study of religion greatly downplay the Transcendent, and think that religion must be studied wholly in a scientific or objective way. (A particularly zealous and learned exposition of this approach can be found in Wiebe, 1999.) They hold that scholars must not let theological views infect the discourse of the study of religion.

This is an eccentric and culturally conditioned viewpoint. It accepts the Western Enlightenment project whole-heartedly. Thus, it has an engagingly naïve view of the objectivity of scientific studies. As we shall see in chapter 1, this project was lamentably subjective in its often dismissive views of Transcendent reality, whilst claiming a quite spurious objectivity for its prejudices. Hence, an instinctive distrust or dismissal of Transcendence still to some extent infects many of the methodological disciplines that have shaped the study of religion (anthropology, sociology, and psychology, among others).

Many who hold the viewpoint that the study of religion is a scientific discipline are philosophers, unwilling or unable to allow philosophy to engage with history or theology in a creative or even existential way or to test scientific objectivity in the furnace of experience. They often have little sense of the realities of history. The Nazi Holocaust against the Jews was justified on scientific grounds, and was made possible by the new technology that could build gas ovens. It was also justified by a truly appalling Christian theology that dispossessed Jews of their status as a people of God. At its greatest capacity, the camp at Auschwitz held 140,000. Its five ovens could kill 10,000 a day. Maybe two million people died there. I offer this information as an illustration of the fact that religion and science are not theoretical disciplines wholly interpreted within the boundaries of the mind. They need to be mapped out in actual human life and recognised as transformative disciplines, for good and ill.

A deeper knowledge of other cultures might help. India has provided an arena in which philosophy and theology are not separated one from the other in the way that they were among a male élite in Classical Greece. Furthermore, the University of Al-Azhar was founded at Cairo in 972 CE as a mosque-university. The ideal in medieval Islam was always that a study of Transcendence is an endeavour to grasp the truth. Similar aspirations have been expressed in many of the world's religions. Even if this has not always worked out in practice, a naïve commitment to scientific methodology as an adequate replacement for God will not do. Nor is the study of the methodology of religion an adequate substitute for seeking to understand and even to harness religion's transformative powers.

The perspective that would keep the study of religion quite apart from confessional commitment also demonstrates a lack of common sense. To study religion without taking commitment to Transcendence into very careful consideration as at least potentially a real concern seems daft to many people. It is like trying to understand cricket as though it is not a sport. You could make the case that: cricket provides a decorative background for a picnic; it encourages the creation of green space in urban wastelands; it has contributed to a decline in family life since it takes up so much time in a player's life that could otherwise be spent with his wife and children; and you could no doubt build many other castles of the mind. One would still be left with the impression that nothing of importance had been said about cricket. In fact, all of us view the

world from where we stand; even those who claim to adopt a
severely rational, logical and objective stance. What matters is the
generosity and humility that enlarge our outlook. I think there is
much wisdom in my revered mentor Geoffrey Parrinder's
observation that it is often faith that best understands faith.
Certainly, it would be foolish to ask a tone deaf woman to
communicate the joys of music, or a man who cannot add up to
explain the beauty of mathematics. Why therefore should we
expect an atheist or agnostic, or even an interested bystander, to
offer a more profound guide to religion than one who is entranced
and caught up by its many and various expressions?

Questions of methodology are of great importance in the study
of religion, and we shall briefly allude to some (for example, the
question of empathy as an adequate human and religious response
to 'otherness') in this book. Yet this is a beginner's guide. Books by
Whaling, Wiebe and others in the bibliography should take any
interested reader further than we shall travel. A wise, witty,
controversial and alluring criticism of religion as a *sui generis*
phenomenon, unique, unexplainable, and largely immune to outside
criticism, is given in McCutcheon (details in the bibliography). Still,
his pointed barbs do not undermine my conviction that faith is an
important focus of the meaning and end of religion. For myself, I
have grave reservations about certain aspects of current
methodological approaches to the study of religion, and about the
shape of the debate about what constitutes religious studies, but
these must largely be dealt with in another work.

Because this book is written out of a particular viewpoint that
transcendence matters, I have occasionally obtruded myself on the
narrative. I hope this is not too impertinent and irritating to the
reader, and apologise if it is. I have done so when it seems necessary,
but have avoided it where possible. In chapter 5, I include reflections
from making radio programmes, so have felt it best to personalise
the narrative there, at several points.

mundane matters

Since this is a beginner's guide to religion, I have kept notes to a
minimum. In the text, I have sometimes, in brackets, pointed the

reader to authors and to the dates of particularly relevant books by them, whose titles can be found by consulting the bibliography. The bibliography points interested readers to a selection of books that will take their exploration of religion further and deeper than I have attempted here. Wherever I have mentioned dates, the references are not to the various religious calendars but to before and after the Common Era (CE for 'Common Era'; BCE for 'Before the Common Era'). Most religions have their own dating systems, but increasingly their members refer to their faith-specific calendars for internal use, and employ the Common Era dating in the public domain. Because this follows the Christian system of dating (though shorn of the confessional use of BC, 'Before Christ', and AD, 'the year of the Lord') it may be that this system will be replaced by some other more obviously neutral system of dating. But for the moment it is widely used by scholars of religious studies.

One last point. Religions are sometimes among the most hierarchical (the origins of that word comes from one meaning 'priesthood') and sexist of institutions. (Certain expressions of religion, however, can be quite the opposite.) Some of the most exciting movements sweeping through contemporary religion are liberationist and egalitarian; though other religious people often resist them, very occasionally for good reasons. I have tried to avoid sexist language, either by using inclusive language, or else when appropriate by using he and she interchangeably.

what is religion?

The answer to the question 'What is a religion?' seems obvious. A religion is: Hinduism, Buddhism or Jainism; Judaism, Christianity or Islam; Confucianism or Shinto; one of the primal, original faiths of humankind, still found in Africa, North America and elsewhere; or one among other self-contained systems of faith.

If, however, we remove the indefinite article and ask 'What is religion?', matters are less clear. Then we are dealing with a much more amorphous phenomenon. So we need to distinguish religion from the religions, before we ask in more detail how they are inter-related. Thereafter, we shall explore whether there is more to the question 'What is *a* religion?' than first one might think.

religion

We begin with religion, not a religion. The word 'religion' derives from the Latin word *religio*. This had a variety of interconnected meanings. Originally, it seems to have referred to fear of or reverence for God or the gods, then later to the rites offered to them. Indeed, there is some confusion about whence *religio* originates. It may come from *relegere*, 'to gather things together' or 'to pass over things repeatedly'. If so, that would indicate religion's concern for, some would say obsession with, establishing rites and rituals and reflecting on past precedent and customary practice. However, most scholars think that it derives from *religare*, 'to bind things together'. That would emphasise religion's communal demands. Religion is not just personal piety, though it is that too, but draws people into common rites, practices and beliefs.

Just as the original meaning of the word *religio* is shrouded in mystery, so is the significance of the earliest human expressions of religion. Certainly, the religious history of humankind begins from earliest times. Evidence suggests that prehistoric humans believed in an afterlife: for example, red ochre was used to stain bones in some Neanderthal burial grounds about 150,000 years ago, probably for ritual purposes. Moreover, cave paintings, for example at Lascaux (c.15,000 BCE) and Ariège (12,000–11,000 BCE) in modern France, seem to indicate a reverence for the world around, and may have been part of a relatively elaborate complex of rites. From 3000 BCE onwards, the rituals of religion are clearly to be observed. Around that date, Sumerian poetry (Sumeria was part of ancient Babylon, modern Iraq) laments the death of Tammuz, the shepherd god. Stonehenge, in the south of modern England, may date from c.2800 BCE; the reason why it was constructed remains mysterious to us. Even earlier than Stonehenge, by about a thousand years, a large prehistoric grave was constructed on the banks of the Boyne River in present-day County Meath, north-west of Dublin, Eire. Indeed, it is a much grander monument than Stonehenge, constructed by an unknown group of people long before the Celts came to Ireland. The 'royal' graves at Ur in modern Iraq and the pyramids and sphinx at Giza outside modern Cairo were built about 2500 BCE. These are more clearly religious in their purpose: for example, the pyramids indicate that by this stage the Pharaoh was a god-king in Egypt; he was the primary focus of the pyramid, which was built to foster his eternal cult.

Thus it was that by the middle of the third millennium BCE, the work of human piety was clearly recorded in art and architecture. Sumeria and Egypt were perhaps the first places where this began in a relatively systematic way, at least with materials that have survived the passing of many centuries. There is also evidence from China about or just after this period.

What did this phenomenon of religion intend to achieve? Nowadays, it is unfashionable to interpret religion from a single perspective. Indeed, it is unwise and misleading to do so if thereby the great diversity of religious phenomena is played down or even ignored. Nevertheless, I attach particular significance to the conviction that religion points to a phenomenon beyond itself and this mundane existence: to what theists would call God; though Buddhists, many Hindus and others would use different terminology.

All major religions believe that there is more to life than meets the eye. The five senses of sight, hearing, smell, taste and touch scan and interpret this mundane existence. Sometimes for humans the penny drops and another transformative and Transcendent dimension opens up to them. The following chapters will take up the implications of this intuitive insight and its consequences. For the moment, it is sufficient to make the point that from very early times, humans have understood there to be a mysterious depth in life, beyond the traditional senses, to be scanned by insight rather than sight, and enabled by prayer and meditation not just the optic nerve. Alongside this recognition of a Transcendent and mysterious reality, there grew up a conviction that humans could relate to it. So, as we shall see in later chapters, the concern of religion has not simply been with a remote 'force' or reality. Rather, humans are embraced within its concerns and commitments. Indeed, some religious traditions prefer to designate that reality as 'him', 'her' or 'them', to impute personality analogous to human understandings of that term.

It is important not to reduce the importance of that Transcendent dimension in religion. It is certainly true that religion has been used to justify social, economic, political or other concerns. For example, the pyramids were no doubt built for a variety of reasons. Probably, the pharaohs Cheops and Khafre intended to strike awe into their subjects for themselves, as well as for the gods of Egypt. Withal, this does not eliminate or even reduce the Transcendent dimension to which religion points.

Yet, in the modern Western world, there has grown up the assumption that the Transcendent dimension to religion can be dismissed as a fantasy of people who knew less about reality than we now do. The contemporary malaise of religion in the West is not a new phenomenon, though it has been a very minority position in the history of the human race. There was a strand of scepticism in the classical Greek and Roman worlds. According to Plato, Protagoras had observed in the fifth century BCE that 'man is the measure of all things'. He was reportedly banished from Athens and his book burned in the marketplace for his repudiation of the city's gods. He observed: 'About the gods, I do not have [the capacity] to know, whether they are or are not, nor to know what they are like in form; for there are many things that prevent this knowledge: the obscurity [of the issue] and the shortness of human life.'

Centuries later, Edward Gibbon, in his *The History of the Decline and Fall of the Roman Empire*, wrote that:

> The various modes of worship, which prevailed in the Roman world, were all considered by the people, as equally true; by the philosopher, as equally false; and by the magistrate, as equally useful. (Gibbon, 1910, p.53)

This wry definition, however, tells us at least as much about the strands of eighteenth century English society Gibbon inhabited or aspired to belong to, as it does of the world of high and late Classical Antiquity. Indeed, the modern and postmodern European world has provided many sceptical definitions of religion. A particularly amusing interpretation was offered by Ambrose Bierce in his *The Devil's Dictionary*, begun in 1881: religion is 'a daughter of Hope and Fear, explaining to Ignorance the nature of the Unknowable'. (It is, of course, undoubtedly true that the heart of religion is unknowable if the only accepted tool of knowledge is unaided human reason, but this is excessively reductionist.)

the origins of religion

The decline of religion in the West can be illustrated by the nineteenth century quest for the origins of religion. Nowadays, most unbiased and fair-minded scholars of religion acknowledge that it is impossible to discover the origins of religion: both in the sense of detecting the earliest moment when religion began; and in uncovering what that moment signified about the intention and truth of the religious life. The impossibility of finding the beginnings of religion, and what it then meant, is because religious origins lie in the swirling mists of prehistory, before writing began and even before artefacts were made that could have survived the erosions of time. Yet most exponents of the quest held that they could explain the origins of religion as arising from a non-Transcendental source.

Despite the impossibility of the enterprise, in the late nineteenth century there was a quest among some European scholars to locate the origin of religion. Why was this project undertaken? It was part of a wider exploration about the origins of humankind and what it means to be human.

In fact, this pursuit was deeply influenced and even driven by a fashionable scepticism about the existence of God or of any Transcendent dimension or dimensions to life. Many such scholars assumed that, although people expressed religion with reference to such a reality, in fact their rites and even beliefs really reflected other concerns within their societies and groups. Very often, its proponents assumed that the origins of religion, when they were located, would explain religion as a wholly human-centred occupation, explicable as an important component in the lives of primitive people but unworthy of the commitment of educated and rational modern humans. Thus, this quest was far from being an objective search for knowledge.

One problem for the credibility of religion in the modern West is that many secular people assume that such a quest has been objective and 'scientific' despite the overwhelming evidence to the contrary, some of which we shall shortly examine. Many who pursued this investigation were founders of the relatively modern disciplines of sociology, anthropology and psychology, or were originators of great political movements like communism, or exponents of the developing physical sciences. Figures like (for example) Spencer, Tylor, Freud and Marx are rightly held in great esteem. But that admiration should be given for their achievements in (respectively) sociology, anthropology, psychology and the political sciences, not for their speculative and unreasonable opinions about religious origins or about religion itself.

A landmark in this endeavour to discover the origins of religion was the publication of *On the Origin of Species by Natural Selection* by Charles Darwin (1809–82) in 1859. This book sought to explain the origins of humankind from the viewpoint of 'evolution'. Darwin was not himself an important figure in locating religious origins but his work encouraged others to observe everything to do with the process of being human from an evolutionary perspective.

The first significant figure to interpret religion from this viewpoint was Herbert Spencer (1820–1904). The contemporary Comparative Historian Eric Sharpe has perceptively written that Spencer's major contribution was to establish evolution as less a theory than an 'atmosphere' (1975, p.34). In Spencer's *First Principles*, published in 1862, he moulded the development of (among other phenomena) society, language and law to an evolutionary framework. He tended to regard religion, not so much as an entity in itself as an aspect of how society is organised and governed. Spencer was hostile to the Transcendental claims of religion. Late in his life, in 1904, he trivialised the Christian view of God as belief in 'a deity who is pleased with the singing of his praises, and angry with the infinitesimal beings he has made when they fail to tell him perpetually of his greatness'. In a more measured moment, he had earlier proposed that 'the rudimentary form of all religion is the propitiation of dead ancestors, who are supposed to be still existing, and to be capable of working good or ill to their descendants' (Sharpe, 1975, p.33f.). This unsubstantiated assertion was to have a long and often discreditable history.

The French philosopher Auguste Comte (1798–1857) invented the term 'sociology', and Herbert Spencer's text *Social Statics* was its first major work (these two scholars are counted as 'fathers of social science'). However, Émile Durkheim (1858–1917), by birth a Jew then briefly a Roman Catholic but an atheist by conviction for most of his life, has had the most impact in establishing, in many people's minds, the interpretation of religion as, above all else, a social fact. Durkheim defined religion as 'a unified system of beliefs and practices relative to sacred things, that is to say, things set apart and forbidden – beliefs and practices which unite into one single moral community called a church, all those who adhere to them' (Sharpe, 1975, p.84). These beliefs and practices sustain and prolong the identity and life of the community committed to them. They are given authorisation by being underwritten and sanctioned by a supernatural being or beings. However, such beings are in reality not as important as the clan or other social grouping, by which they are created in the senses and the imagination as forces for social cohesion. The gods therefore have no ontological reality; in other words, they do not exist as independent realities, but are social constructs created to explain or even mould the way individuals behave in society. Durkheim put it like this in his *The Elementary Forms of Religious Life* (1913): 'In a general way a society has all that is necessary to arouse the sensation of the divine in minds, merely by the power that it has over them; for to its members it is what a god is to his worshippers.'

Durkheim located the beginning of religion in the totemism practised, so he held, by the Australian aborigines, whom he believed were an example of the earliest human social system. In his view, the totem has a mysterious power (*mana*), which punishes violations of *tabu*, which is the sacred in its most basic form. He interpreted the totem as a symbol serving two functions: it is a symbol of the tribal god or gods; and it is also a symbol around which tribes gather and by which they identify themselves. In Durkheim's view, because the totem serves both functions, it shows that god and totem are alternative expressions of the collective group, of society. He held that in more advanced, modern societies, dogmas and rites are prescribed for the faithful by 'society', which separates all things into the two categories of *sacred* and *profane*.

Durkheim's view of totemism was deeply indebted to the work of the anthropologist William Robertson Smith (1846–1894), who was rightly criticised by some of his contemporaries for seeing totemism everywhere. He located it, controversially, behind biblical sacrifices. He believed that when sacred animals were sacrificed and eaten, their meat and blood bonded them to their worshippers. Among others, Max Müller, about whom more below, was highly sceptical of this interpretation.

This tendency to view religion as embodying the rather infantile practices of 'primitive' people characterised much early anthropology as well as sociology, and continued well into the twentieth century. When the distinguished Christian Comparative Religionist Geoffrey Parrinder (b.1910) first went to West Africa in 1933, two groups of Western people actively disparaged ancestral faith there: some Christian missionaries and, especially, anthropologists. Parrinder set about challenging their views. Chapter 2 of his book *West African Religion* (1949, p.11–17; Forward, 1998a, pp.74–82) severely criticises the works of distinguished anthropologists, especially Lucien Lévy-Bruhl (1857–1939), for creating and reinforcing the notion of a universal 'primitive religion'. Lévy-Bruhl was certainly among those who used anthropological data to argue that primitive peoples' thought was qualitatively different from that of modern humans. He believed them to be prelogical, unable (for example) to separate cause from effect, thus conceiving the universe differently from lettered people. Although he did not describe them as illogical, it was a short step for

others to take that they were innately inferior to civilised human
beings. Such anthropologists lumped African tribes together with
Australian aboriginal groups although, in Parrinder's view, many of
the former had progressed far beyond the totemistic conceptions of
the latter.

Parrinder also had stern things to record about the word
'fetishism' as an adequate description of West African religion. This
word was introduced by the Portuguese who called the African
charms and cult objects *feitiço*, meaning 'magical', and was
popularised and made respectable by Auguste Comte. Parrinder
deplored the fact that it lingered 'in the mind as a handy, but
undefined and therefore practically useless, description of queer
practices in Africa . . .(and) still appears in some books on religion
and anthropology. . . (and) is still commonly employed by too many
missionaries'. In his view, words like fetishism, juju and gree-gree
'need to be relegated to the museum of the writings of early
explorers'.

Parrinder had kinder things to write about Edward Burnett
Tylor's (1832–1917) introduction of the word animism as a good
step forward from fetishism, because it acknowledges a spiritualistic
rather than materialistic view of the world which lies beyond objects
of reverence. In 1884, Tylor was appointed Reader in Anthropology
at the University of Oxford, the first such post ever to be established
(between 1896 and 1909 he was the university's first Professor of
Anthropology). He defined religion as 'the belief in Spiritual Beings'.
He borrowed the term 'animism' from a German chemist, Georg
Ernest Stahl (1660–1734), who held that all living things derive
from *anima*, 'soul' or 'mind'. Tylor located 'animism' in the current
'atmosphere' of evolution, and employed it to depict the culture of
humankind progressing from lower to higher forms, for the most
part in an unbroken flow. Animism is the earliest form of religion,
and can be studied through 'survivals' from the past. Hence, one can
study surviving 'primitive people' to understand how ancients must
have lived and organised their social customs and ways of life
(Sharpe, 1975, pp.53–58). Parrinder believed that animism, though
an improvement upon other anthropological terms, was basically a
dismissive word employed by unbelieving and alien scholars. He
wrote that: 'To talk of animism would reduce religion to a system
based on a delusion, the supposition that there is personality or life,

in or behind objects that, in the view of European science, have not got them.' In other words, Parrinder was inclined to think that anthropologists in his heyday and a little before it had overlooked the most obvious source of the meaning of religion: that is, belief in a God who actually exists and relates to human beings, who can experience his will and even his nature in this present life.

There are now interesting attempts by scholars of religious studies to integrate anthropology into the multi-disciplinary field of religious studies; for example, a brave attempt has been made by Clinton Bennett to do so (1998, *passim*). However, they often fail sufficiently to understand and overcome the lingering scepticism that many modern anthropologists have inherited from their nineteenth century ancestors. There are still indications that many anthropologists fail to understand the claims of its adherents that religion fundamentally witnesses to a Transcendent rather than to a human or social reality, even though it may cast light on these areas. For example, although anthropologists working recently in West Africa are far less secular-minded than they were, many still play down the Transcendent element of traditional religion (Forward, 1998a, pp.73–97). For this reason, scholars of religious studies need to refract other perspectives, including anthropology, through the basic religious assumption that there exists a dimension to life beyond the remit of secular disciplines. Later in this chapter, we shall explore how this might be done, by looking at Jesus' parable of the Prodigal Son.

Early sociologists and anthropologists assumed that the structures of human society and beliefs actually express only a 'this-worldly' perspective of what it means to be human. What, however, of the claim that humans can relate to that Transcendent reality? Can the origins of religion be located there? Rudolf Otto (1869–1937) was one of two impressive figures who helped shift the emphasis away from primitive beliefs to that of primeval religious experience. He was a Professor of Systematic Theology, first in Breslau and thereafter at the University of Marburg from 1917 to 1929. He had visited India in 1911–12. Notions of Christ or Christianity as the fulfilment of Indian religious experience were then becoming commonplace: significantly, J.N. Farquhar's *The Crown of Hinduism* was shortly afterwards to be published (in 1913). Although this branch of Christian theology magisterially conformed other ways of faith to its own interpretation of truth, it did at least posit or imply an innate if ill-defined capacity for spiritual growth in all humans. This emphasis was influential upon Otto.

An even more powerful experience upon Otto was a trip he made to a synagogue in Tunis. There, hearing the words of the Jewish prayer about holiness, he experienced a deep sense of wonder, drawn forth by an impression of the numinous, the *mysterium tremens et fascinans*, a tremendous and fascinating mystery. In Otto's *The Idea of the Holy* (1917), he wrote of this 'non-rational' or 'suprarational' core of religion. He called it the 'numinous', from a Latin word meaning a supernatural entity. The numinous communicates a sense of awe and otherness. It arises out of faith, rather than being rationally demonstrable. Indeed, Otto's contention was that the holy or the numinous cannot be described or defined but only 'evoked' or 'pointed to'.

William James (1842–1910) has been as influential a writer as Otto in the realm of religious experience. His *The Varieties of Religious Experience* (1902) stresses the individual's religious life rather than social expressions of religion. He coined the phrase 'stream of consciousness' to introduce his readers to a wide range, or perhaps deep flow, of religious experience. His pragmatic perspective emphasised the fruits of religion, not their doctrinal foundations. He understood conversion in a psychological way as breaking through to a form of consciousness that fully realises the 'spiritual Me'. However, this is only one of the ways to realise the 'spiritual Me'. The other, possibly more common route, is by the 'once-born' cultivation of the healthy-mindedness from childhood through adulthood. James was to have an important impact upon other psychologists who were not always as sympathetic to an interpretation of religion as expressing a real phenomenon as were Otto and James.

One of the most important of these sceptical figures was Sigmund Freud (1856–1938), a giant figure in the emerging school of psychoanalysis. He depicted the role of religion in individuals and societies in a largely disapproving way. His *Totem and Taboo* (1913; English translation 1917) asserts rather than argues that the beginnings of religion, ethics, society and art meet in the Oedipus complex. This phenomenon is the repressed sexual desire for the mother by a male child, which sets up a rivalry with the father. Indeed, in Freud's view, all neuroses have their origin in introverted and sexual childhood experiences, so religion must be bound up with some repressed experience in the childhood of the human race. His *The Future of an Illusion* (1927; English translation 1928) develops his argument that religion is a collective expression of neurosis, an attempt by people to escape from the realities of an unfriendly world. They seek this comfort in the illusory world of fantasy, in a God and a heaven that are mere projections but have no independent reality. Although anthropologists largely dismissed Freud's views as an expression of capricious irrationality, like many other nineteenth- and early-twentieth-century scholars of religion he assumed an evolutionary framework for the development of religion. Even so, whether in its primitive or more advanced forms, for Freud, each stage of religion's evolution still betrays its status as a beguiling yet false interpretation of how things really are.

Yet Freud has pertinent warnings for the religious person. His most important book, *Civilization and its Discontents* (1930), written late in life, describes mystical experiences in terms of an 'oceanic feeling' of 'oneness with the universe' which arises from the helplessness of childhood and is especially pronounced in the religions of India (1982, p.9f.). Within this rather superior comment by a European about phenomena of which he knew nothing of importance, understandable in the imperialistic context of his day, lies the important point that religion can be nothing more than a childish fantasy or illusion. Most of us know religious people whose faith is immature or even abusive. Yet one may wish to argue against Freud that faith, if expressed in infantile fashion by some people, may be more developed and integrated in others. Freud makes the mistake of describing religion at its worst rather than its best.

the age of nationalism and internationalism

The nineteenth- and twentieth-century Western view of religion as an inappropriate option for civilised human beings grew up in the context of massive political, social and economic changes on the continent of Europe. As the earliest sociologists, anthropologists and other pioneers of the human sciences were articulating their new ideas, the world around them was in flux. The changing times deeply influenced their developing conceptions.

In mainland Europe, the revolutions of 1848, though not initially successful, brought a form of constitutional government to France (though that soon faded away) and even shook the Hapsburg throne of the Austro-Hungarian Empire. That same year, there was a revolt in Rome. The papal premier, Count Rossi, was assassinated and Pope Pius IX (whose pontificate lasted from 1846 to 1878) fled to Gaeta.

In 1870, the Prussians defeated the French in a series of battles. The French Emperor Napoleon III went into exile and the Second Empire was replaced by the Third Republic. The following year, King Wilhelm I of Prussia was proclaimed Emperor of Germany at Versailles, near Paris in France. Meanwhile, Italy was gaining its freedom and unity at the expense of the papacy, which had hitherto ruled much of the Italian peninsula. In 1870, Italians entered Rome and named it their capital city of a united country. Pope Pius IX retreated behind the walls of the Vatican. The reforms of the first Vatican Council that year, which promulgated the dogma that, in certain matters and on certain occasions, the pope could speak infallibly, can be seen, historically, as a conservative and essentially anachronistic response to the massive political changes that the papacy had to face. In fact the great years of papal political power and influence after which Pius nostalgically yearned were centuries past.

England had had its more modest share of social upheaval some years earlier. The Great Reform Bill of 1832 had extended the franchise to the upper-middle classes. Four years later, the Chartist movement demanded universal suffrage and vote by ballot; it could be claimed that this was the first national working-class movement in Great Britain. Thereafter, political, social and economic reform tended to be evolutionary rather than revolutionary.

The point is that the age of nationalism, inaugurated by the French Revolution, swept through nineteenth-century Europe. It brought in its train tantalising glimpses of a more liberal form of government, placing people rather than their rulers at the centre of things, holding out the hope to each person of citizenship of a state in place of being the subject of a monarch. At the risk of overstating matters, it could be said that many progressive people in nineteenth-century Europe preferred to be subject to the brotherhood of man rather than to the fatherhood of God. For in these tumultuous times, religion, specifically the Christian religion, often seemed to be part of the forces of reaction rather than of reform. It was no doubt for this reason, among others, that academics who sought after the origins of religion often did so in the assumption that the phenomenon of religion had become an anachronism. For them, its real meaning lay in the mists of time, in prehistory, and its relevance was now over.

Probably the most famous critique of religion in the nineteenth century is that found in the works of Karl Marx (1818–83), the German social and political theorist. His searching criticisms of religion arose from his conviction that the real meaning of religion lay beyond itself in the aspirations of the socially and economically oppressed. In his view, religion may originally have had certain positive features. Specifically, it may initially have been a real attempt to revolutionise society and abolish exploitation. Yet its failure to do so made it otherworldly rather than this-worldly. Thus, the religious life is symptomatic of unfulfilled human existence. People attempt, in their religious life, to have in fantasy what, in reality, they do not possess: affirmation, hope, love, faith in the future and so on. The idea of God expresses the reality of social alienation. Once the ills of society are remedied, then religion will wither away. Even before the revolutions of 1848, Marx had written his most famous statement, in his *Critique of Hegel's Philosophy of Right*, published in 1844:

> Religion is the sob of the oppressed creature, the heart of a heartless world, and the soul of soulless conditions. It is the opium of the people. (1970 edn., p.131)

For Marx religion had become an oppressive structure, since it supports the governing classes, which it suggests are placed there by divine will. Marx's ideas were much indebted to the work of Ludwig Feuerbach (1804–72) whose theory of projection was widely influential (notably upon Freud, as well as Marx). Simply put, in relation to religion this means that in worshipping God, people are worshipping themselves.

Marx's importance was in the way others used his ideas to change the shape of society. He is the father of communism, which has usually been virulently anti-religious, and which dominated the ideological beliefs of much of the world's population from the October 1917 Revolution in Russia until the fall of the Soviet

Empire in the late 1980s and early 1990s.

Unsurprisingly, given Marx's analysis of religion, for much of the twentieth century avowed communists and milder socialists have regarded that phenomenon with great suspicion; not just Europeans of Christian or Jewish origin, but others of a different religious background. For example, Jawarhalal Nehru, the cultivated first Prime Minister of independent India (from 1947 until his death in 1964) and rather an upper-class socialist, wrote in his marvellous book, *The Discovery of India*, that:

> We have to get rid of that narrowing religious outlook, that obsession with the supernatural and metaphysical speculations, that loosening of the mind's discipline in religious ceremonial and mystical emotionalism, which come in the way of our understanding ourselves and the world. (1956, p.552f.)

Nehru, although from a Hindu background, was very much a secular rationalist who, as an adult (he joined the Theosophical Movement at age thirteen), in terms of religion favoured an eccentric interpretation of the Chinese way (*Tao*) of ethical endeavour tinged with religious scepticism (1936, p.377). Yet he and other socialists and Marxists might have taken on board the criticism of Marxism by Sigmund Freud, himself no friend of religion, that:

> The writings of Marx have taken the place of the Bible and the Koran as a source of revelation, though they would seem to be no more free from contradictions and obscurities than those older sacred books. (In his *New Introductory Lectures on Psycho-Analysis*, 1973 edn., p.217)

criticisms of the secular quest for the origins of religion

In recent years, telling criticisms have been made of the project of searching for the origins of religion as it has been pursued by such secular and sceptical writers as we have briefly brought forward. Many non-Western writers have seen with particular clarity the fundamental lack of evidence that sustained many if not most of these theories. A contemporary Turkish Muslim scholar, Adnan

Aslan, has written that:

> the quest for the origin of things, including the origin of humankind,
> the origin of the universe and the origin of species, has left a legacy of
> the so-called scientific method for intellectual generations to come...
> It is my view that such attempts to explain the nature and the origin
> of religion have simply created a body of theories which are diverse
> and, in some cases, conflicting. (Aslan, 1998, pp.31, 29)

This is well put. The scientific method (as Aslan somewhat
imprecisely calls it) is a rather blunt instrument with which to
uncover the meaning of religion; and, indeed, may often be an
inappropriate or at least a relatively unimportant one. Furthermore,
this sceptical quest for the origins of religion was not as scientific as it
looked.

A few distinguished scholars took part in the quest as people of
religious faith. Even they did so on excessively theoretical grounds.
This can be illustrated from the works of the great Max Müller
(1823–1900), one of the few scholars of religious origins who paid
the phenomenon of religion the compliment of assuming that it
might reflect a reality rather than a delusion. He was indeed an
extraordinary scholar (Chaudhuri, 1974, *passim*); in fact an
historian of religions, who coined the term 'the scientific study of
religion' in his *Chips from a German Workshop* (1867), and the
major pioneer of the comparative study of religions. A German
scholar, he moved to Oxford in 1848, where he spent the rest of his
life and was eventually appointed Professor of Comparative
Philology in the university. He became a naturalised Englishman
who wrote fluently in his adopted language. Among his many works
were an edition of the Rig-Veda (the oldest of the Vedic collection of
Hindu hymns, dating from about the thirteenth century BCE) and
forty-nine volumes of *Sacred Books of the East* (1879–94). To this
day, he is greatly and rightly honoured in India, though he never
went there but instead learned of its religious and cultural life in the
Bodleian and other libraries. His aphorism about the science of
religion, 'he who knows one knows none', found in his *Introduction
to the Science of Religion* (1873), has been widely quoted and has
much force. Even so, it should be remembered that he had little
experiential knowledge of other faiths. Unlike him, most people do
not work out and deepen their religious life in libraries.

Müller was much influenced by Enlightenment principles, and held that all human knowledge begins with the apprehension of finite entities, registered by the senses. Yet he believed that these imply more than themselves; they point to the infinite. Religion begins when a moral sense joins that sense of the infinite. This 'Natural Religion', the bedrock of all forms of developed religion, is 'the perception of the infinite under such manifestations as are able to influence the moral character of man' (Sharpe, 1975, p.39). Müller was especially persuaded and influenced by the philosophy of Immanuel Kant (1724–1804), whose *Critique of Pure Reason* he translated in 1881. He believed that religion is the capacity of all humans to perceive the infinite. Accordingly, all religions contain in some measure the eternal verities of belief in God, the immortality of the soul and a future judgement. Müller's (debatable) conclusion that religion originated in India gave him a sentimental attachment to that area though, as we have seen, he did not feel any practical responsibility to visit it.

He was a true romantic. (Indeed, he was the son of a minor, sentimental German poet whose works live on because the great composer Franz Schubert set certain of them to some of his greatest music.) His idealism separated him from early anthropologists and sociologists, since he believed that even early humans had an innate capacity to apprehend the sacred. He was not persuaded that ancestor worship, social bonding or any other imputed explanation of the meaning of religion could explain away this instinctive, intuitive grasp of the sacred. Müller believed that this intuition was not a special revelation but was gained simply by an appropriate exercise of human reason; though he may have believed in a primal revelation that underlay this act of rationality. Greatly to his credit, he was suspicious of some of the more outlandish notions about primitive people. On one occasion, he told Darwin that the history of language was the history of thought. Just as there was no half-developed language, so there could not have existed 'partly rational, partly developed men'. The men parted, agreeing to differ.

Müller was unusual among many contemporary scholars of religion in being a Christian, in later days a member of the Church of England on the somewhat questionable ground that 'I think its members enjoy greater freedom and more immunity from priestcraft than those of any other Church.' He realised that, in retaining a belief in the importance of religion for his own day and age, he was out of step with most scholars of religion. In his *Lectures on the Origin and Growth of Religion* (1878), he wrote that:

> Every day, every week, every month, every quarter, the most widely read journals seem just now to vie with each other in telling us that the time for religion is past, that faith is a hallucination or an infantile disease, that the gods have at last been found out and exploded. (1882, p.224)

Müller was hardly an orthodox member of England's established church. He was, philosophically, a nineteenth-century Western idealist, interpreting the 'truth' of a phenomenon by its faithfulness to its origins. So he believed that the Hinduism of his day was a sad debasement of its Vedic ideals. This, however, betrays both his idealistic philosophy and his text-based rather than experiential interpretation of religion. He portrayed Christianity as top of the ladder of religions, but possibly looked for a future more perfect evolution of a religion that would embody humanity's greatest repository of truths.

Indeed, Müller's work often betrays a speculative as much as a rational, evidence-based foundation. For example, he argued for the fundamental importance of solar mythology, asserting that heroes and gods were in origin solar metaphors. In this, he almost deserved the facetiousness he attracted: one wag marshalled 'evidence' to prove that Müller himself did not exist but was in fact a corrupted solar myth. Müller's work also illustrates the tendency of many such scholars to deduce much from little. From his discovery that the Sanskrit word Dyaus is philologically equivalent to the Greek word Zeus, he concluded that India was the original home of humanity, from where languages, beliefs and myths were dispersed.

Andrew Lang (1844–1912) was an important critic of Müller, believing that the origins of religion are shrouded in mystery. He noted that many primal tribes have the conception of a Supreme Being who exists alongside other spiritual agencies like dead ancestors and other supranatural forces. This view is still current among many scholars of African traditional religions. A Roman Catholic priest, Wilhelm Schmidt (in *The Origin and Growth of*

Religion, first published in 1912), a less precise scholar, located an original High God in the primal consciousness, which later became modified (or even degenerated) into a belief in many deities.

A much more recent 'faith-full' explorer of the origins of religion has been the great promoter of what is termed 'history of religions', Mircea Eliade (1907–86). At one level, he sounded the death-knell of this quest. In his *Australian Religions* (1973), he wrote that:

> Western scholarship spent almost a century in working out a number of hypothetical reconstructions of the 'origin and development' of primitive religions. Sooner or later, all these labours became obsolete, and today they are relevant only for the history of the Western mind. (1973, p.xv)

Yet at another level, his own views were dependent upon a somewhat romantic theory of origins. He wrote that: 'The history of religions shows that we are not just biological cousins of the aboriginals, but friends and collaborators on a common human destiny.' He interpreted religion as the manifestation of 'Being'. Against the sceptical scholars a generation or two before him, he argued that the human being is *homo religiosus*; that is, motivated by an essential religious purpose. He looked at archaic cultures, and believed that they provided evidence for the 'morphology of the sacred'. He held that modern humans have suffered a new Fall (commensurate with the fall of Adam and Eve from the paradisal garden, as described in the biblical book of Genesis, chapter 3) by marginalising ritual and relegating myth to the unconscious. Thereby they destroyed a sense of the sacred. Whereas people in a premodern society could attain spiritual heights by using symbols to relate to and live in the universal, highly cultured moderns are spiritually deeply impoverished, and cannot afford to be as 'profane' as they are.

Eliade was much dependent on the work on religion and the unconscious by Carl Gustav Jung (1875–1961). Jung had emphasised the importance of archetypes as the patterns or symbols of the collective unconscious. Eliade wrote that:

> The world of the archetypes of Jung is like the Platonic world of Ideas, in that the archetypes are impersonal, and do not participate in the historical Time of the individual life, but in the Time of the species – even of organic Life itself. (1960, p.54)

It is as if archaic people live in their archetypes whereas modern humans have fallen out with theirs. The result is clear for all to see: including a foolish dependence on progress; and an inability to understand or overcome evil (Smart, 1975, pp.213–17). A dialogue between the modern and the archaic person needs to happen, so that Western humans can rediscover their own souls. Eliade criticised his predecessors for their dismissive interpretations of religion. Yet he was as guilty as they were of mistaking an ideological theory about the past for findings based on hard evidence.

the end of the quest for the origins of religion

Looking back from a contemporary perspective, it is remarkable how many unsubstantiated claims about the origin and function of religion have been widely offered and accepted as self-evident truths, which emphatically they are not. (For example: assertions about the practice of totemism in Australia; and about religion originating in ancestor worship or even in patricidal fantasies.) Furthermore, late-nineteenth- and early-twentieth-century scholars of the origins of religion simply took evolution for granted as an obvious explanation for how phenomena developed. Only the carnage of the First World War from 1914 to 1918 caused it to be questioned and then eventually abandoned or at least seriously modified as an explanation for how things come to be.

Despite a widespread abandonment or modification of a theory of evolution, some of these assumptions of the earlier quest about the supposed explanations for religion linger in the popular and even the educated mind. In particular, there is a widely held scepticism in the West about the meaningful existence of God or some other supranatural being, beings or state of being. I employ the adjective meaningful, because statistics often indicate that a majority of people in the West believe in God, but many of them find it difficult to describe any momentous or even minor practical consequences to their opinion.

Nowadays, with rare exceptions (e.g. Masuzawa, 1993, *passim*), it is not fashionable to search for the origins of religion. Even so, it would be foolish of contemporary religious people to condemn outright all of the aims and achievements of the quest for the origins and meaning of religion. To be sure, it was afflicted by a sense of cultural and even racial superiority that the political environment of Western Imperialism in which its exponents lived did nothing to dispel and much to instil. Further, it paid lip service to an academic methodology that was all too rarely followed. Ironically, as Eliade indicated, it was the human ideas about religion that were illusory, not necessarily religion itself.

Such disciplines as sociology, anthropology and psychology arose in a confused and haphazard manner, and were hardly as objective and scientific as many of their early spokespeople claimed and believed. At bottom, many of their pioneers held that religion was more a human than a divine product. Indeed, many asserted or assumed that the human mind and spirit wholly manufactured it. Of course these disciplines of the human sciences have been refined by successive generations of scholars. But their legacy of relatively uninformed agnosticism or atheism lingers on in the Western mind.

Religion has often been displaced by secularism, scientism, or some other ideology in the contemporary West as the primary source of humankind's explicit or implicit loyalties and hopes. The proponents of these dogmas have often displayed that prejudice masquerading as knowledge that many of them condemned in the tenets of religion. For example, certain philosophers, sociologists and anthropologists have placed modern humans in a pecking order, with rational, sceptical Westerners at the top and others much lower down. The Englishman James Hunt (1833–69), President of the newly-formed Anthropological Society, declared in 1863:

> that the Negro is a different species from the European; that the analogies are far more numerous between the Negro and the ape than between the European and the ape; that the Negro is inferior intellectually to the European; that the Negro can only be humanized and civilized by Europeans. (Haddon, 1910, p.79)

This was during the American Civil War (1861–5), which was fought, to a great extent, over the issue of black slavery. Hunt's words are a reminder that the secular disciplines were not value-free, 'scientific' pursuits, but were used to justify practices like enslavement and imperial subjugation by a 'master race', practices that are now rightly condemned. Secular disciplines can be just as imperious and domineering in their claims as religion; and just as destructive, if not more so.

the place of religion in society

Even if the Western world has not quite displaced religion, it has largely separated it from the fabric of society. This means that religion can easily be regarded as an optional extra. Hitherto, in the vast majority of times and places religion could best be regarded as part of the warp and woof of society. Now it has become detached from the texture of Western culture, displaced from its position within an earlier unitary view of existence. This is not so elsewhere. I can illustrate this in a personal way.

Some years ago, I went to a small village in Pakistan for three weeks in order to improve my knowledge of Urdu, that country's national language. (By and large, only Urdu and Punjabi were spoken in the village, although a few people had a smattering of English and a very few communicated well in it.) The village was wholly Muslim. Some Hindus and a few Sikhs had lived there before partition in 1947, but they had left for India at that time. People were curious why I, a Christian and not a Muslim, should want to be there. When they learned that I was a committed Christian and not anti-religious as many assumed that I, a Westerner, must be, they confided to me many of their own convictions. One young man took me to his mother's grave, and told me how important faith had been in her life and how she had taught it to him. He said his prayers whilst we were there, unembarrassed by my presence. Another young man took me to the graves of two men who had died many years before. The elder man was a *pir*, a spiritual guide whose teaching is still followed and whose intercession with God is still sought by many villagers today. The son was also a *pir*. Many people in the village and from all over the surrounding areas come to the graves. Barren wives arrive (one or two whilst we were there), tie little 'flags' to the overhanging tree, and pray for children. Others, men, women and children, come and pray for what they most earnestly desire.

In a village where religion is part of the fabric of everyday life, people have a matter-of-fact attitude towards and relationship with

A grave in Paurmiana, the small Pakistani village visited by the author in 1985

it. Islam prescribes five daily prayers. Clearly, many people did not follow this regulation, though some did. Most seemed to pray from time to time. Many Muslims the world over, and also in that village, refer to the tradition (hadith) of the Prophet Muhammad that 'between a person and unbelief (*kufr*) is the leaving of prayer'. Yet this does not seem to mean that people punctiliously observe all the religious law's injunctions about prayer; rather, that believing Muslims will at least pray sometimes, and very often (if they are men) communally at midday on Fridays. Every adolescent boy and man turned up for the weekly Friday lunchtime prayer in the mosque. It seemed that religion was simply there, a dimension of life to be taken more or less seriously, unquestionably an integrated part of everyday life. For myself, the most interesting moments were when I shifted from observing as a fascinated outsider to participating as though I were an insider. By this, I do not mean committing myself to the faith and practice of Islam but rather living as though the rites and conventions of religion were not absent from or marginal to daily life, but simply there, to be seized and used.

The best example of this happened when I left the village for a day. I returned from my destination rather late. I caught the last train back, and had no great hope of making the necessary connections thereafter to get me 'home'. When I got to the nearest railway station to the village there was one horse and cart there. I took it as far as the owner would go. Near where he dropped me there was a hut. A man came out and, recognising me, offered to take me to the village, still a considerable way off, on his scooter. I accepted gratefully. Throughout the journey, my Western Enlightenment convictions were in abeyance. I knew this was the daftest trip I had ever made, with dacoits (robbers) in the area, yet was sure that I was safe in an enchanted world. My point here is not to compare worldviews, nor to suggest that my sense of safety was either sensible or misplaced. It is to say that, for a while, I saw freshly, as others saw; not from my usual perspective.

I had lived abroad before, but not quite like this. I was removed from the phone, from linguistic fluency, from running water. I was far from other people like me: my culture, religious commitment, and race were different and marked me out as such. I was deskilled and often unnerved. Even so, I experienced moments of quite extraordinary Transcendent luminosity. I learned to live in a world in which it was assumed that religion was part of the warp and woof of society, not an intrusive and old scrap of material that did not quite fit the evidence of the senses.

There were some indications that religion could be destructively totalitarian. One young woman and her mother took me to a part of the village where Hindus had lived before the partition of the sub-continent in 1947. Then they were chased out. The mother told me she had had friends there, but had joined in harrying and expelling them. She told me: 'Those were difficult times. Why did we do what we did, in the name of God and religion? I don't know.'

Usually, however, in that village, religion had not been totalitarian. The unusual circumstances of independence, when Pakistani politicians made religion the focal and unifying point of the new country's identity (though the reasons for partition were many and various, not the least of them being economic), momentarily caused engulfing chaos, wide-scale movements of religious populations, violence and death. Even so, the creation of Bangladesh out of Pakistan in 1972 revealed that religion, if it is torn from the wider fabric of society, cannot by itself sustain the lives of communities. Languages, common histories, social networks and several other factors are important perspectives which, if ignored, come back to readjust decisions taken on monolithic grounds.

The matter-of-fact attitude towards religious observance in that village reminded me that religion is not simply or, indeed, mainly (in spite of Max Müller's convictions) the sound knowledge and application of religious treatises. Nor is the religious figure who often represents the literary-based dogmatic claims of religion (the imam of the mosque, in this case) always taken as seriously by believers as he would like to be; nor should he be, since he represents only one facet of religion not its totality. Religions are more internally diverse than many such interpreters admit or even know. Often, too, they are profoundly influenced by other neighbouring religious worldviews. For instance, the fact and the form of Hindu practices of the veneration of holy people and sacred places have richly and profoundly affected both popular and mystical Islam in South Asia. An example of this is the veneration of the *pirs* in the Pakistani village where I stayed. This kind of popular or folk Islam has been deeply influenced by Hindu devotion to holy men and women. Many Muslims hold that it is forbidden to seek human intercession with God (e.g. Quran 2:255 appears to frown upon it). Most Muslims who practise this popular form of Islam are from its majority Sunni branch (which forms about ninety per cent of all Muslims). Some of their (often self-) appointed representatives inveigh against these religious customs in the name of an orthodoxy that is not as uniform or as totalitarian as its custodians would like it to be. In fact, the veneration of holy men who are friends of God is a very common practice by Muslims throughout India and Pakistan and in other places too.

Indeed, if religion is most often a dimension within different societies and cultures rather than a displaced phenomenon, then it should be expected that the social norms and practices of each context will affect the form each religion takes; just as the religion will influence other dimensions of that culture. So Islam has a very different 'feel' about it in Saudi Arabia, Pakistan, Morocco and Indonesia. Sometimes, the dimension of religion in society is not the most important one, even when religious enthusiasts would wish and claim otherwise. Some years ago, a leader from the North-West Frontier Province declared that 'I have been a Pakistani for forty years, a Muslim for fourteen hundred years; but a Pathan [the major ethnic group of that area] for ever.'

Here, surely, is where other perspectives, like sociology and anthropology can genuinely illuminate how religion functions in different cultures. An example may be given from the earliest days of one of the great world religions in order to illustrate how sociological and anthropological perspectives cast light on religious meanings. Jesus told the parable of the Prodigal Son (Luke 15:11–32). It is about a young man who asks his father for his share of the property. When he receives it, he goes abroad and squanders it. Eventually he returns, tail between his legs. To those who first heard this story, it would be shocking for a father to make a spectacle of himself by running to greet and embrace his returning wayward younger son. This is particularly so in the society in which Jesus lived, where all three characters in the story offend against the concept of honour of a Mediterranean village society. There is a fond and foolish father who divides his estate. There are two shameless sons who accept this shocking decision, which could, in such a time and place as first-century Galilee, imply that they wished he were dead. At the end of the story, their scandalised neighbours would, by coming to the feast held by the father to celebrate his younger son's homecoming, have accepted both back into the solidarity of the community. Yet what of the elder son? He accuses his brother of squandering money on prostitutes, though the story has not previously indicated this (the NRSV's translation, 'dissolute living', in verse 13 is mistaken; the Greek *zon asotos* means 'living wastefully'). He therefore slanders his brother and publicly insults his father; as the elder son, he should have greeted the guests, not stayed away, sulking. At the end of the story, he is the one who is marginalised by his shameful behaviour. And what of the mother? The story is puzzlingly silent about her. What did she think of her sons' actions? And of her husband's? What was her status in this dysfunctional family, and the effect of its problems on her acceptance in the community at large?

Even on a more traditionally 'religious' reading of the text, there are some nice incidental points to shock the conventional hearer: for example, a Jewish boy, at the end of his tether, is reduced to working with 'unclean' animals like pigs. Furthermore, it is a very matter-of-fact view of repentance that makes the young man return to his father on the grounds that even his father's hired hands are better off than he. His pretty little speech to his father about having sinned against heaven and before his father is a rather shabby way of ingratiating himself, rather than a statement of deep penitence. Indeed, the term 'repentance' is never mentioned in the story. An important emphasis of the parable is that the lad has no idea of the depth of his father's love, who is interested only in the fact that he has returned, not in the reasons for it. Elsewhere, the evangelist Luke (who alone records this story) shows an interest in the sincere repentance of sinners (for example, in the story of Zacchaeus in chapter 19 verses 1 to 10), but not here. The emphasis is on the father's shocking love, mirroring God's abundant grace for undeserving sinners. This ought to make the hearer puzzle over the real meaning of repentance. Even if, as with Zacchaeus, it implies a change of heart and direction of life, it requires a hard-headed appraisal of the advantages that accrue from such a decision.

To some hearers, this somewhat calculating, self-interested, unsentimental view seems rather shocking. Yet in the context of Jesus' peasant and artisan society (and no doubt that of Luke's rather different original audience, which was possibly slightly more rich and bourgeois in attitude than the author thought was good for it), struggling to survive and flourish in a colonial context and at the mercy of good harvests, religion was not a hobby but an essential and power-giving perspective. This story of Jesus manages both to challenge and subvert social expectations, yet also to indicate that within ordinary life and its constraints, generosity and forgiveness can break through and be signs of God's kingly rule (Shillington, 1997, pp.141–164; Forward, 1998b, pp.76–78).

Above all, this story illustrates my conviction that religion's primary function is to witness to a Transcendent dimension.

Anthropological and sociological understandings of the ancient Mediterranean world genuinely illuminate how Jesus' original hearers (and Luke's first readers and listeners) would have understood his teaching. By a process of comparison and contrast, we can understand how different are concepts of parenting, family responsibilities and so forth in large parts of the modern world. Yet wherever that story has been read and preached, it has touched human hearts with a piercing insight into Transcendent grace and goodness, in whatever cultural garbs it has been clothed. Religion must use the resources of secular disciplines to illuminate its message but not be captured and subsumed by them.

religions: a modern invention?

We have established that religion is deeply rooted in human history and prehistory. What, however, is the link between religion and the religions? Are religions simply culturally appropriate ways in which religion expresses itself? On this view, Hinduism is the natural religion of India, Confucianism of China, and so on.

There is some truth in this notion but it is easy to see its drawbacks. The expulsion of Hindus from that village when Pakistan was created out of British India as a homeland for Muslims shows how easily religious sensibilities can be exploited to emphasise differences, to the point of rejection and even destruction. The fact that exactly a quarter of a century after partition, in 1972, Bangladesh was carved out of Pakistan indicates that linguistic, regional and national aspirations are as important, more important sometimes, in creating social cohesion than religious affiliation.

One important and hugely influential pioneer of the meaning of religion and the religions has been the contemporary Canadian scholar, Wilfred Cantwell Smith (1917–2000). Most of his books since his ground-breaking *The Meaning and End of Religion* (first published in 1962) have drawn out and built upon its conviction that if we are truly to understand the religious traditions of humankind, we should not reify them. In his view, the West has made a mistake in 'mentally making religion into a thing, gradually coming to conceive it as an objective systematic entity' (1978, p.51).

An example of this mistake was when Europeans turned the many expressions of faith in India into the entity of Hinduism, a term unknown in South Asia before the Europeans came. This imposed a false unity upon a variety of significantly different ways of rites and practices.

Smith adds a sterner charge against those who would reify religion: 'Fundamentally it is the outsider who names a religious system... The participant is concerned with God; the observer has been concerned with "religion"' (1978, pp.128, 130). Yet even if it is the case that (for example) Hinduism was designated as such by outsiders who were part of an intrusive imperial system; and even if such an appellation homogenises and over-simplifies complex and overlapping phenomena in the name of a single entity; the word 'Hinduism' still usefully describes a generic phenomenon. But, like all words that describe religious systems, it is a word with fuzzy edges. For example, it is surely possible to detect broad similarities between the (often profoundly) different 'schools' of thought in South Asia. For sure, it is sometimes difficult to draw a line between these variant schools and other ways of faith that are arguably so different that they constitute separate religions. There are some Hindus who include the ancient religions of Buddhism and Jainism, and the relatively modern religion of Sikhism, within the Hindu religion. One straightforward reason for not drawing a line in this case is that most Buddhists, Jains and Sikhs would disagree with that assessment.

As the beginning of this chapter put it, a religion is: Hinduism, Buddhism or Jainism; Judaism, Christianity or Islam; Confucianism or Shinto; one of the primal, original faiths of humankind, still found in Africa, North America and elsewhere; or one among other self-contained systems of faith. Yet these self-contained systems are not rigidly watertight. The boundaries are fluid, and some of the traffic between the religions deeply influences not just the periphery but the heart of other faith-systems.

Members of some religions claim that that nomenclature is inappropriate for the system to which they belong. It is not uncommon to hear Hindus and Muslims claim that they belong to a way of life. Yet often, what these people are denying is the Western compartmentalisation of religion, reducing it to one (sometimes unimportant and optional) branch of life. Or else there is a polemical edge to their claim: you belong to a religion, they seem to be affirming, whereas I follow the way of truth, salvation, liberation or enlightenment.

religion as systems

What may be difficult but is crucial for the Western mind to grasp is the concept of what I would call the fluid boundaries or fuzzy edges of religions. The Enlightenment world can cope with subjects and objects, you and me, us and them. This is a point of view that happily deals with clearly defined boundaries. Reality is rather differently and often more appropriately conceived elsewhere. I suggest that we should regard religions as structures or systems that are fluid, in two senses. First, they interpenetrate with other dimensions of reality, such as politics and economics, within the various contexts in which they are located. Secondly, religion itself unlocks its secrets to those who recognise its pluriformity. It cannot be reduced simply to belief or good behaviour, or any other solitary interpretation.

It may be that another way of explaining religions as phenomena with fluid boundaries can be found by following the advice of the philosopher Ludwig Wittgenstein (1889–1951). He held that it was wrong to search for the essence of a phenomenon that would enfold everything in that category. Thus there is no definition of religion that all religions can agree upon: for example, many religions emphasise the concept of a creator God, but Buddhism and Jainism (among others) do not. Yet in other important ways, these two phenomena count as religions. Although it is always pleasing to call an eminent philosopher as a witness, simple common sense would also indicate that, for all their differences, the world's religions are identifiably such: that is, religions.

In recent years, there has been some notable work done in the area of the importance of the religions as systems, particularly by John Bowker, a significant yet still somewhat underrated contemporary writer in this area. Unlike Wilfred Cantwell Smith, Bowker has few problems with accepting the concept of religions as embodying how things really are. He defines religions as 'organized systems which hold people together'. This leads him to ask why such systems are necessary. His answer is that religions 'are the earliest cultural systems of which we have evidence for the protection of gene-replication and the nurture of children'. Just as the skin is the first defensive boundary of the gene-replication process, so culture is the second defensive skin in which the gene-replication process sits. It does not matter that our earliest ancestors knew nothing of how gene-replication works, since successful practice, rather than understanding, guarantees survival within the evolutionary process. Religions are highly organised protective systems for the survival of, but also to give meaning to, the human race. Even today, more than three-quarters of the world's population is affiliated to some religion, however loosely.

This still leaves the important query, why should this human system of gene-replication be a *religious* one? As Bowker rather neatly puts it, 'animals, birds and fish live in many different kinds of social organizations without saying their prayers (so far as we know, though some religions have thought otherwise)'. His explanation is that the possibilities of the emergence and development of religion are latent in the human brain. Humans are genetically *prepared* for religion, as they are for (for example) sleeping, eating and drinking, and linguistic aptitude. This gene-protein process does not determine what humans will do with this preparedness. Which is why there is much that is universal and common in religious behaviours but also why there are crucial differences among them: because what people in different cultures do with their preparedness is not determined. Bowker suggests that the person in the crowd who held up the sign 'Prepare to meet thy God' should actually raise one that reads, 'Prepared to meet thy God'.

Religions have been successful because they are flourishing protective systems tied to the potentialities of the brain and body. Because they are thriving, people who are attached to them are set free to explore their own nature and that of society around them in confidence and security. The structures of religion (for example, gods, guides and gurus; holy book and places; the apparatus of sangha, church or whatever, among many other things) give people an environment within which life can be lived as a project: to discover the meaning and end of life. (Bowker, 1995b, *passim*; Bowker, 1997, pp.xvi–xxiv).

This definition of religions as systems, if true, builds upon some of the sceptical nineteenth- and early-twentieth-century sociological, anthropological and psychological theories of the origin and meaning of religion. Yet, with the aid of contemporary scientific insights into what it means to be human, it gives a more positive interpretation of religion. Whilst it is true that religions are social entities, that concern human values and the workings of the human mind, nevertheless religion may be an essential, genetic component of being human.

Bowker's definition of religions as systems offers hope for the future of religion in the West. Preparation for religiosity is so deeply embedded in the human brain that such capacity for reverence will not just go away. However, he admits that it could atrophy by non-use. Even more likely is that if 'real' religions disappear, some form of inferior ersatz versions will take their place. Aspects of the New Age movement in the West may already point in that direction.

At least two criticisms can be made against the definition of religions as systems. The first is whether there is in fact, to put it very crudely and simplistically, a religious gene. No doubt, time will shortly help us to determine this, given the rapid pace of growing (though often disputable) knowledge in this area of scientific research. The second is that, if Wilfred Cantwell Smith is too eager to question the existence of religions as real entities, believing them to reflect the impetus of the modern Western mind towards dividing and pigeon-holing existence into discrete categories, Bowker sometimes seems to fall into the (almost opposite) trap of making the boundaries of religion too rigid and determined.

My own tentative preference, recognising the enormous contribution both scholars have made to the debate about religion and the religions, is to emphasise what I have already argued for: religions have fuzzy edges; and (though this is not a perfect metaphor) they are best regarded as one of a number of interrelated perspectives within each social setting. The distinguished British anthropologist Mary Douglas (b.1921) has argued that the primitive worldview (still true for primal societies in the modern world) is more holistic than that which dominates the contemporary West:

The different elements in the primitive worldview are closely integrated; the categories of social structure embrace the universe in a single, symbolic whole. In any primitive culture the urge to unify experience to create order and wholeness has been effectively at work. In 'scientific culture' the apparent movement is the other way. We are led by our scientists to specialization and compartmentalism of spheres of knowledge. We suffer the continual break-up of established ideas. (Douglas, 1991, p.57)

If she is right, then despite the experience of most people reading this book, religion has most often been interpreted by humans, not as an optional extra within each culture, but as an essential component that interweaves closely with other perspectives in order to confer and sustain meaning for people in society.

empathy for the religious other?

Smith, Bowker and Douglas write as believers, unlike many authors on religion a generation or two before them. Is it possible to be empathetic towards the beliefs of others, whilst maintaining a proper scholarly impartiality? Some proponents of 'the phenomenology of religion' have thought so. This approach to the study of religion is indebted to the concepts of philosophical phenomenology developed by Edmund Husserl (1859–1938). The religious phenomenologist rejects reductionist explanations of religious phenomena. She also puts on one side any evolutionary or other framework that would involve making value judgements. Rather, she aims to filter out the distortions and prejudices that have imposed meaning upon religion rather than drawn meaning out of it. To filter out these imposed assumptions, she adopts the process of what Husserl called *epoché*, 'bracketing'. She must 'bracket out' her beliefs and judgements about the value or otherwise of particular phenomena, and instead impartially observe the experience itself. Then she must adopt the method of *einfühlung*, empathy, in order to understand the religious other. Using *epoché* and *einfühlung* as two methodological tools, she can comprehend the essential structures of the aspect of religion under observation, or even of religion itself. Husserl referred to this comprehension as 'eidetic vision'; *eidos* is Greek for 'essence'. Thus intuition and insight, rather than experience of rational thought, enable the phenomenologist to understand the 'essence' of religion.

A number of distinguished scholars of religion have developed this concept. For example, Ninian Smart has argued for what he calls 'methodological agnosticism'. This means the enquirer should presuppose neither acceptance nor denial of the truth of Transcendent 'otherness' in his investigation into religious experience.

This method has a number of advantages but also several serious drawbacks. In its favour is the desire to understand from the inside. Had nineteenth-century seekers after the origins of religion held such a view, they might have had more humility about the capacity of others to discern a reality they so easily spurned. Yet their lack of humility can be easily paralleled by the exaggerated claims some outsiders have made about their capacity to grasp and perceive what others experience. Can they really do so? Even if we marry into another culture, speak another language and try our best to empathise, can we really see as others see? And even if we can, what use do we make of it? It could be argued that Shakespeare's character Iago is an empathetic figure. He insinuates himself into Othello's psyche, perfectly understands his strengths and weaknesses, and takes advantage of them so as to destroy him and his wife, Desdemona. Scholars who make much of empathy as a positive concept in interreligious understanding (they include, in the bibliography, Smart and Markham among others) need to do more than assert it as a valuable tool. They need to explain its possibilities as a positive concept in an era of globalisation.

Frank Whaling offers a resounding defence of the phenomenological approach. He argues that:

> Its basic intuitions concerning the need for suspension of judgement, empathy, and non-judgmental comparisons remain sound . . . [Its intention]. . . is not to get inside the conscious view of believers in a literal sense but to understand them in such a way as not to give offence. (Whaling, 1995, p.20)

Maybe, then, Whaling is arguing for appreciation more than for empathy. David Brown was Bishop of Guildford and the first Chair of the British Council of Churches' Committee for Relations with

People of Other Faiths. He used to tell how deeply, as a scholar of Islam and friend of Muslims, he felt his exclusion from Friday prayers in a mosque when he was a missionary in the Sudan. He was told that, despite his friendships with Muslims and deep knowledge of and high regard for Islam, he did not have the right 'intention'. He was so near, yet so far from the faith of others. Another scholar of Islam, Clinton Bennett, is a more confident phenomenologist. He writes of virtual insidership, drawing on the insights of a former colleague, Philip Meadows. They recognise that what is achieved is an approximation of an insider view rather than its realisation, yet Bennett's is a very confident nearness. He tells us that his home is bicultural, English and Bengali, and suggests that it is only conversion that would prevent him from being an insider; indeed, his Muslim friends cannot understand why someone who knows so much about Islam can remain a non-Muslim (Bennett, 1998, p.8–10). Later in his book, with less certainty but arguably greater insight, Bennett writes about Muslim conversation partners appreciating his interest in and knowledge of Islam (1998, p.197). This seems to me a more positive way forward. My own experiences, including that of living in a Pakistani village, incline me to believe that what one can achieve are friendship, respect and appreciation; these are more easily attainable than insidership and empathy, and arguably more valuable. Certainly friendship gives glimpses, perhaps even broad vistas, of what it looks like to see through another's eyes, even to the point of virtual insidership; but it is easy to be arrogantly over-confident about our capacity to discern and interpret the meaning of the faith of others. I agree with Wilfred Cantwell Smith that we should attempt to realise what it is like to belong to another religion. Yet I would argue that this is an aspiration never wholly realisable.

None of us is, in fact, wholly free from presuppositions or able to bracket them out. Indeed, phenomenology's two methodological tools of *epoché* and *einfühlung* are contradictory. The first is, in intention, objective, whereas 'eidetic vision' is very subjective. Indeed, the study of religion, at its most exciting and insightful, treads a difficult route between these two poles. It should aim at a fair and impartial understanding of the faith and practices of divers peoples. Yet we should also recognise that many scholars of this discipline have religious convictions of their own. They are not dry and desiccated observers, but caught up in the excitement of this vibrant subject.

the perennial philosophy

There have been many attempts to locate the heart of religion. As we shall see in further chapters, some have seen religion as primarily the teachings of a founder, whilst others interpret it as a mystical experience with Transcendent reality, and another group locates it primarily as obedience to an ethical code or religious law. These are inherently reductionist approaches, which attempt to interpret the essence of religion as fundamentally one part of its variegated forms.

Some of these attempts have crossed religious boundaries, and have been held by very distinguished scholars, though this does not necessarily make them convincing or compelling. A particularly influential attempt is the *philosophia perennis*, or perennial philosophy. This has been popularised in English by a book of Aldous Huxley (1946, *passim*). In earlier years of this century, it was associated with the Hindu scholar, Ananda Coomaraswamy, and the Muslim savant Frithjof Schuon, and even with the great Roman Catholic scholar of Islam, Louis Massignon. More recently, the Muslim Seyyed Hossein Nasr and the Christian Huston Smith have held it with particular clarity. Huxley described this philosophy as:

> The metaphysic that recognises a divine Reality substantial to the world of things and lives and minds; the psychology that finds in the soul something similar to, or even identical with, divine Reality; the ethic that places man's final end in the knowledge of the immanent and transcendent Ground of all being – the thing is immemorial and universal. (1946, p.1)

The perennial philosophy teaches that outward aspects of the world's religions are diverse and often even contradictory. However, the inward aspects point to a single absolute. In the cosmos, the one (Absolute) becomes many (phenomena) through a series of hierarchical levels, through which the individual can ascend to the truth. The path on which he travels necessitates him embracing the outward form as well as the inward meaning of the religious tradition he espouses. Advocates believe that the perennial philosophy is very old, found in humankind's earliest primal experiences of faith, as well as in the great religions of the modern world.

The perennial philosophy is a seductive interpretation of the world's religions. It offers, in a rapidly secularising world, a sense of the sacred that lives within all the religious traditions, a wisdom to which all humans therefore have access. Further, it allows for, indeed insists upon, each human committing herself to a religious path, rather than picking and choosing bits from each faith as do some advocates of the New Age or Postmodernism. The sacred wisdom of the perennial philosophers may be compared to a fountainhead gushing forth water at the top of a hill. The streams flow their independent courses down the hill. They do not meet and mingle on their routes, but rather their underlying unity is in the source. So there may be many outward differences and contradictions between the faiths, many fundamental divergences of beliefs; yet there is a fundamental absolute from which they draw their resources to inspire and make wise *homo religiosus*, the religious human.

It would be possible to criticise this interpretation of human religiosity as Gnostic. Gnosticism is the belief that some people claim to have an innate, superior knowledge of spiritual realities. To be sure, many religious people have a tendency to regard this phenomenal world as quite unreal in comparison to the inner world of Transcendent reality, to the point where some Gnostic approaches can be dismissed as world-denying asceticism. Yet this criticism of the perennial philosophy can be overstated. Much Gnosticism does not deny the world but rather relativises it in terms of the Transcendent dimension beyond the five senses. It is precisely a strength of certain forms of Gnosticism, including the perennial philosophy, that it insists that there is more to life than meets the eye. This 'more' must, they insist, be taken very seriously indeed. Furthermore, proponents of the perennial philosophy could claim that they take very seriously commitment to Buddhism, Islam, Christianity or whatever is their spiritual home, and indeed may argue that it is more approximate to the demands and even nature of the Absolute than are others of its manifestations. Yet they maintain that an understanding of the eternal Absolute is a healthy corrective to our myopic obsession with the demands of the present and the particular.

Even so, proponents of the perennial philosophy often write in a magisterial way. One can either affirm or disbelieve their points of view, but it is almost impossible to argue with them, since they assert rather than make a case for their position. Indeed, they assert too much, and argue their case too little. Indeed, they seem to find abstract philosophical thought easier to cope with than historical realities. For example, the very different Christian and Muslim assessments of Jesus, arising out of the different revelatory sources of both religions, are hardly reconcilable by the use of historical tools (Forward, 1998b, pp.124–136). That difference continues to cause difficulties to dialogue between the two faiths. Yet it seems better to provide an ethic for coping with difference rather than arguing that such profound historical and scriptural differences matter little at the level of the Absolute. A second and related criticism of advocates of the perennial philosophy is that, although they find space for all religions as fashioners of truly religious people, they do so by downgrading the importance of religions. Religions are the lowest level in the hierarchy. Moreover, many such scholars find it difficult to avoid criticising religious systems to which they do not belong. For example, Nasr implicates Christianity in the Western trend towards agnosticism and atheism.

The perennial philosophy usefully reminds us of a profound, universal spiritual dimension to life. Yet it may be that mysticism or some other phenomenon can provide a better understanding about the Transcendental unity of the religions. Or it may instead be the case that we should not reflect the diversity of religion through a single prism, but rejoice in its profusion and its many and elaborate forms. If so, then we can understand religion better by providing a model or models that emphasise the importance of its multi-faceted nature, rather than by employing a model that, in practice, reduces variety to a unity that convinces only its proponents and other like-minded people.

how to recognise a religion

A number of distinguished contemporary scholars have offered various characteristics of how we might 'see' or 'identify' a religion. Perhaps the most influential such model has been that proposed by Ninian Smart. Professor Smart's definition of the nature of a religion contends that each has seven dimensions: the practical and ritual dimension; the experiential and emotional dimension; the narrative or mythic dimension; the doctrinal and philosophical dimension; the ethical and legal dimension; the social and institutional dimension; and the material dimension (1998, pp.11–22). This has proved a fruitful way of describing the world's religions and has been a useful educative tool for many teachers of religious studies.

Professor Frank Whaling has offered a slightly different approach, worth quoting in full:

> In the first place, all the major religions of the world contain eight inter-linked elements. The major religions are dynamic organisms within which there are eight interacting dimensions; they are historical chains within which there are eight connecting links. The eight links are those of religious community, ritual, ethics, social involvement, scripture/myth, concepts, aesthetics and spirituality. All religions have some sort of religious community, they all engage in different forms of worship, lying behind them are certain ethical norms, they are all involved in social and political outreach within the wider community, sacred texts and myths are important for them all, they all emphasise particular clusters of doctrines, they all produce religious art and sculpture, and they all infer distinctive modes of spirituality. In other words there are eight common elements within the great world religions and it is a great help to be aware of this for they provide pegs upon which knowledge can be hung. (1986, p.38)

Both these models are useful for teaching purposes. However, although these models help to focus our understanding of religions, they do not exhaust their pluriformity. One must not mistake a teaching aid for the whole of what it attempts to define and convey! Furthermore, they betray a rather Western, modernist rather than postmodernist, perspective on religions as primarily objects of investigation rather than as homes for the human spirit, though Smart and Whaling certainly do not neglect this dimension of their importance in their writings.

In this regard, the work of Eric Lott provides a useful corrective. He argues for a core vision within each religion that is then interpreted in a variety of ways to convey Transcendent reality to believers (1988, *passim*). By focusing upon this visionary core, Lott reminds students of religion that they are not simply engaged upon an objective, academic enterprise but upon humankind's oldest quest; a journey of transformative power. True, Lott could be faulted for over-simplifying the visionary core of each religion. It may well be that there are visionary cores within each religion. Nevertheless, his important work deserves widespread appraisal.

In the following chapters, I offer my own route through the complex foliage and forests of religion. As I indicated in the Introduction, we move from exploring, in this chapter, 'What is Religion?' to chapter 2, which asks 'Is anyone or something there?' This explores the deep-rooted notion in the human heart, mind and spirit that there is more to life than meets the eye. Chapter 3, 'How the Transcendent sees us and we see the Transcendent', illustrates how people throughout the centuries have attempted to understand, interpret and respond to that dimension to life that is, in some ways, more than meets the eyes. Chapter 4 is entitled 'The Good Life'. It describes what religions demand of their adherents in terms of an orientation towards the world. Chapter 5, 'Religion in the New Millennium' looks at the challenges facing religion in the contemporary world, and hazards a few guesses about its future importance.

It is important to recognise that this framework intends to give an impression of major concerns of the religions, past and present. It does not aspire to summarising the heart of religion in a reductionist way. However, this book does have a contention: as I wrote in the Introduction, I attach particular significance to the conviction that religion points to a phenomenon beyond itself and this mundane existence. Many authors of the academic models of religion admit the importance of Transcendent reality to a study of religion and the religions, but are careful to indicate that they describe human convictions about that reality without committing themselves to a point of view as to its truth.

However, I want to claim that faith in that Transcendent power's capacity to engage with humans and transform them is the most exciting base from which to engage in a study of religion and religions. I do not quite claim that this is the heart of religion, since many religious people do not actually believe in the objective existence of Transcendence or at least do not trust in its interest and involvement in the human enterprise of living and dying. I find myself on the side of those scholars who openly recognise and affirm the importance of the visionary core of religion. I am not persuaded by the views of those who disbelieve, or even those who think it possible and desirable wholly to lay aside one's own convictions in order to study religion in an objective way. I guess that some reviewers may find a lingering (but I hope positive and not narrow) influence of my Methodist Christian commitment in this book. So be it. Religion is too exciting, demanding and even shocking to reveal its secrets to those who aspire after a bloodless objectivity.

is anyone or something there?

Creator of the germ in woman,
Maker of seed in man,
Giving life to the son in the body of his mother,
Soothing him that he may not weep,
Nurse (even) in the womb,
Giver of breath to animate everyone that he maketh!
When he cometh forth from the womb…on the day of his birth,
Thou openest his mouth in speech,
Thou suppliest his necessities.
When the fledgling in the egg chirps in the shell
Thou givest him breath therein to preserve him alive…
He goeth about upon his two feet
When he hath come forth therefrom.
How manifold are thy works!
They are hidden from before us
O sole God, whose powers no other possesseth.
Thou didst create the world according to thy heart.

(Appleton, 1985, p.13)

This is a prayer of the fourteenth century BCE Egyptian Pharaoh Akhenaten to Aten, the sole God. This pharaoh may have been the first person in human history to establish the cult of the worship of one God whom he worshipped as Aten, the light that is in the sun, which brings the world into being and sustains it. Akhenaten moved the capital of Egypt from Thebes, at the juncture of Upper and Lower Egypt, to the new capital, named Akhetaten, in honour of this sole God.

Yet this pharaoh won no favours for inaugurating this step forward in the history of humankind, if such it was. After his death (he died, probably murdered, as a relatively young man), his body was either enclosed by a second-hand coffin, or may even have been thrown to the dogs. This was a truly appalling fate for a king who would have expected to have been interred in splendour in the Valley of the Kings (or perhaps in another resting place nearer to the city he had built in honour of his God), surrounded by artefacts to celebrate his glories and hasten his journey through the underworld. His city of Akhetaten was abandoned, and was buried for centuries in the sands of the desert. Its founder was rarely mentioned by his successors, who erased his symbols and figure from monuments wherever they could. If his reign had to be mentioned, he was designated 'that criminal of Akhetaten'.

Why was Akhenaten so execrated? He was accused of impiety, and of offending the deities of Egypt, not least the god Amun-Ra. There was no doubt a strongly political component to Akhenaten's actions. His original name was Amenhotep IV (meaning 'Amun is content'; his new name meant 'one beneficial to the Aten'). His abandonment of the god Amun, whose name he originally bore, was probably partially aimed at destroying the power of its increasingly influential priests. Even so, it is impossible to dismiss Akhenaten's actions simply as political stunts, embarked upon to accrue greater power to himself. The imaginative and reverent power of his prayer speaks for itself. The few artistic impressions that remain of him show him moving away from the stylised grandeur of his predecessors (and of his successors; not least Ramses II a few decades later, whose depictions at Abu Simbel show him towering over friend and foe alike) to greater realism. Akhenaten was an ungainly man, with wide hips and thick lips. He seems to have been a painfully honest man, allowing and even encouraging such realistic depictions of himself.

Akhenaten did not seek to assimilate such deities into the cult of Aten; he was no fulfilment theologian, interpreting the past as leading up to and fulfilled by the sun god. Rather, he repudiated the deities of Egypt's long past, which had sustained her and caused her to flourish for well over one thousand years. His successors held that he had turned Egypt *seni-meni*, 'passed by and sick', and that, under his rule, all 'the deities turned their backs on the land'.

In later generations, many regarded Akhenaten's 'experiment' as religious advancement, rather than as the actions of an erratic and deluded man. It is fascinating to ponder how differently he was regarded by most of his contemporaries than he has been by many since then. The reasons for this contrast may become clearer as we look at the different ways people have interpreted the dimension of Transcendence in their lives. We shall begin by looking at polytheistic views of eternal reality.

polytheism

Polytheism means a belief in many deities. Many nineteenth-century scholars, notably Herbert Spencer, held that this belief was common in the childhood of the human race, and that monotheism was a later development. (Not everyone believed him. In chapter 1, we noted Wilhelm Schmidt's view that the original belief of humankind was in a High God and that this degenerated into polytheism.) Max Müller proposed three stages in humankind's religious evolution. The first stage was henotheistic (a word he possibly made up), when humans worshipped one God without necessarily denying the existence of others. The second stage was polytheistic, brought about by the 'disease of language', the result of humankind's inability to express abstract ideas save by means of metaphors. Finally, there was psychological religion, in which people employ abstract thought to express their devotion to the one God.

We need to be more circumspect and recognise the many and diverse ways in which humans have expressed different views of Transcendence. Sometimes, a variety of views has been held in the same society. Other societies have had more uniformly held beliefs and practices. The capacity to choose ways of being faithful or not, open to many people in the contemporary world, is rather unusual. Moreover, development is not always progress in everybody's opinion. Some changes can be interpreted by many as mistaken, misguided, even wrong and calamitous.

The legacy of a belief in human progress has led many modern scholars of religion to assume that Pharaoh Akhenaten's introduction of monotheism into Egypt was a good thing. But if we stand outside this assumption, then we can see how appalling it must have seemed to many of his contemporaries. Akhenaten disturbed the order and harmony of ancient Egyptian society by his revolutionary rather than evolutionary approach to religious life. His people had long followed a religion that had allowed for the worship of gods and goddesses who performed particular roles and functions in the world of men and women. To many of them, his religious revolution would not have looked like a step forward at all. Rather, it would have seemed a denial of the deities who had sustained Egyptians and Egyptian history for centuries. Imagine that contemporary Jews, Christians and Muslims were told by a very powerful political leader that they had to unify under a God he had discerned who was greater and more real than the manifestations of him that they and their ancestors had worshipped for centuries. How indignant they would feel! How bereft of tradition and identity they would be! If ancient Egyptians felt something of this anger, dread and betrayal, as the chilling response to Akhenaten and his reforms show many certainly did, no wonder that Akhenaten ended up cursed and derided.

Indeed, the view that polytheistic societies are more backward than monotheistic ones is highly questionable, as we shall see in due course when we look at South Asian religious experiences. The myth of monotheism pervades Western culture, to the point that the autonomous independent personality is considered normative and God is likewise often viewed as a kind of superman. The assumption that there should be, for example, one God, one Scripture, one Church, one Son of God or one prophetic-founder is quite simply that: an assumption, not a necessary truth. Polytheism has its own distinctively different insights into how Transcendence impinges upon human hearts, minds and spirits. Perhaps we can locate some of those insights through an imaginative attempt to think ourselves back into the minds of polytheistic worshippers like the ancient Egyptians. Why did they believe what they believed?

Let us examine the story of Isis, Osiris, Seth and Horus in order to explore the alluring power of Egyptian polytheism for its adherents. The story of these deities developed over more than two millennia. Eventually it had three aspects. The first is described in the Pyramid Texts of c.2500 BCE. The god Seth (whose image of a tail with a forked end, a curving snout and two tall ears first appears at the very beginning of Egyptian history, about 3000 BCE) hastened to Osiris in Abydos, killed him, and caused the waters to bear him away to hide his mysteries. Osiris was the god of the dead who had led good lives, not of all of the dead as is sometimes assumed. He seems to have been a new form of an old god, Khentamentiu, whose cult at Abydos in Upper Egypt he absorbed. This early account is reticent about the moment of the murder, but describes the whole cosmos as in chaos thereupon. The gods wept, and their tears turned to materials such as honey and incense, which could be used in the mummification process. (It may be significant that Osiris, as the deity of the righteous dead, enters Egyptian history at about the same time as the process of mummification.) Later accounts develop this story. Osiris's sister and wife, Isis, brought him back to life. The only other consistent feature of the story is that Seth not only killed but also dismembered his brother Osiris. In later times, each part of Egypt was described as home to one part of the god. Nearly three millennia after the first account of the killing, the second century CE Greek writer Plutarch compiled a connected account, but it is more indebted to conventions of Greek storytelling than to earlier Egyptian accounts. To Plutarch we owe the story that Seth tricked his brother into lying in a cedar wood coffin at a feast, after promising it to the man who most nearly fitted it. Plutarch also includes two accounts of Osiris's death and two of Isis's restoration of him to life. Probably this was an attempt at harmonising different versions of the story. Plutarch also recounts that only Osiris's phallus was lost, swallowed by a fish, but Egyptian sources contradict this assertion.

The second part of the story recounts how, when Isis recovered Osiris's body, he impregnated her and then withdrew to rule the underworld. Isis gave birth to Horus. Mother and child stayed in the marshes of the Nile Delta, where she defended him from the forces of evil. Again, this part of the story has many variants and developments but has certain consistent characteristics over a wide span of time and in many texts and representations. Isis runs away from Seth on the urging of Thoth, the ibis- or baboon-headed god of the moon and of knowledge. She gives birth to Horus in Akhbit, and protects her child against snakes and scorpions until he can fight against Seth and claim his inheritance.

The final part of the story records Horus's fight against Seth. It is the oldest part: the linking of Horus and Seth predates the first mention of Osiris by over six centuries. Indeed, the pharaoh in Egypt first appears in textual record as the god Horus. This part of the story has many aspects. Isis plays an ambivalent role, as the sister of Seth but more decisively as the mother of Horus. All participants emerge as damaged. Seth takes the eye of Horus according to the early Pyramid Texts. Horus takes the testicles of his uncle. In one version, Horus is angered by his mother's wavering loyalties and beheads her, losing his eye as a punishment. In another account, Seth rapes Horus to prove his supremacy, which is only overcome when Isis tricks him into eating his own semen. After their clashes, which are not only physical but also appeal to legal argument, there was judgement. At first, both were given half of Osiris's earthly power: some sources indicate the halves as Upper and Lower Egypt; others as the fertile valley and the inhospitable desert. Then Horus emerges as ruler of the undivided kingdom. Until the first millennium BCE, Seth was not utterly cast out of the world by Horus, but retained within it as the destructive and undisciplined power standing alongside the forces of order. Seth becomes defender of the sun god Ra; his disorderly powers ironically fighting off any other chaotic forces that disturbed the serene and immutable movement of the sun through the sky. Horus's vindication before the bar of the deities later developed into an account of the judgement of the dead. Horus leads the deceased to his father Osiris and to forty-two deities who witness the weighing of the dead person's heart. If the heart was filled with goodness then the person was declared to be like Horus, justified by the tribunal, and entered the underworld. Otherwise, the deceased was refused entrance.

From this story, we can draw some tentative conclusions about a polytheistic view of eternal reality. These conclusions must be provisional, since it is all too easy to extrapolate universal truths from particular and local tales. Indeed, it is worth noting that in ancient Egypt, as in many other places and times, some gods and goddesses were found only in one area and never achieved more widespread importance. For example, Mont, the falcon deity, was worshipped in four towns in the province of Thebes. We may guess that this instilled, in the devotees, a pride in their native place, allowing them to be a part of the greater whole of religious and political Egypt yet also rooted in a particular locality. Yet the tale of Isis, Osiris, Seth and Horus raised larger issues, for Egypt as a whole, and (as I shall suggest) far more widely.

The first point to be made is the sheer entertainment of the stories. People would have enjoyed telling and elaborating them. In an oral and aural society (where the spoken and the heard word were of central importance, more so than the written word), they would have been told, retold and pondered. This would have led to their developing interpretation.

These tales would also have unfolded to those who told or heard them, truths about the human condition as ancient Egyptians lived it. The first part of the story, the murder and revival of Osiris, promised the renewal of nature in the present and of life after death. Egypt could only flourish as a civilisation because of the fertile Nile valley, caused by the river's inundation. The story speaks of the rhythms of natural life, of fertility after the waters rise and flood the land; and of the rhythm of this natural life as a mirror of supranatural realities. The second part of the story illustrates the dangers Egyptians faced from wild animals, yet offers the hope that they will escape them. Again, it points to the cycle of life. In a society where infant (and adult) mortality must have been high, Isis's protection of her son was a poignant reminder of the possibilities of the sudden death of close relatives; her success offered hope in the midst of fear and danger. Indeed, it is worth pointing out that Isis is the common thread in the elaborating traditions of this story, from its beginning to its end. It would be trivial to portray Egypt as other than a patriarchal society. Yet it did locate certain roles for women. The female Pharaoh Hatshepsut reigned from 1505–1484 BCE, wearing male dress and a false beard in the depictions that survive of her (her successor Thutmosis III destroyed many of her images). More significantly, the stories of Isis would have enabled women to locate their own lives and its meanings in the drama of Egyptian religious life. The third stage of the story offered insights into the nature of the pharaoh's rule of his two lands, the expectation of the certain yet somewhat equivocal victory of good over evil, and the hope of eternal life for the good person. Lurking behind these issues lie matters of wider resonance for all human beings: the mystery of suffering; mixed human emotions, acted upon, of love, hatred, jealousy, ambition and duty, often in conflict with each other and ambivalently resolved; the power of human sexuality, for good and evil; the instability of life, from which comes the human craving for and pursuit of order and the sense that chaos lies behind even our surest hopes and certainties.

This depiction of life is not, as William Shakespeare wrote many, many centuries later, 'a tale told by an idiot, full of sound and fury, signifying nothing'. Ancient Egypt was not a backward country but a highly developed society. Its glories lasted for centuries, indeed millennia, from the middle of the third century BCE to the dawn of the Common Era. The Roman and British Empires lasted for far briefer a time. The Ptolemaic pharaohs, Greek successors to Alexander the Great who died in Egypt in 323 BCE, made as much use of the pantheon of Egyptian deities as did their predecessors one thousand years and more before them. This usage included resorting to the stories of Isis, Osiris, Seth and Horus. Of course, throughout ancient Egyptian history they were used, and in part were even intended, to buttress political power. Yet modern Western cynicism about the integrity of politicians, and especially about their relative lack of power to order and control events rather than be overtaken by them, should not mislead us to impute similar sentiments to everyone in all civilisations, past and present. We should not forget how important such authority was in ancient Egyptian society, to promote order and defend and sometimes extend Egypt's borders. Pharaohs needed to deliver peace and prosperity, or else suffer unpopularity and even revolt. No wonder that they invoked stories of the deities to emphasise their importance to the wellbeing of their subjects. Equally, it is not surprising that their people were willing to go along with this, at least as long as the king could deliver political, social and economic bounty. Yet the stories are more than apologies for rulers, whether good or bad. We have indicated that they raise important aspects about living in this life, and hold out hope of the next.

Although ancient Egypt aimed to be an ordered society, it was not a static one, though change would often have been gradual and almost imperceptible. The revolutionary ideas of Akhenaten failed to win popular support, yet in a more evolutionary way, the relative importance of deities within Egyptian society rose and fell. Indeed, the god Amun, against whom Akhenaten moved, gained importance in later generations. So the stories of the Egyptian deities can mirror and even give impetus to changes that are taking place in society.

As far as we can tell Egypt never produced philosophers as Greece did from about the sixth century BCE onwards. This means that religion provided a very powerful and largely unchallenged means of understanding the place of human beings within the mysteries of life and death. Any challenge to religion came from other religious perceptions of this life and the next; such as that of Akhenaten or, in a more gradual way, of the developing cult of Amun.

It might therefore be thought that polytheism in a society like ancient Egypt served a different and much less sophisticated function than in a reflective society like fifth-century Athens. In chapter 1, we noted Protagoras's scepticism about the gods. Yet this can be overstated. Only free men in certain city-states of ancient Greece, notably Athens, had the freedom to think and to vote on matters that affected the life of their community. Slaves and women were regarded, in practice, as not fully human. In 1949 CE, Simone de Beauvoir pointed out that from Plato (427–347 BCE) to Jean-Paul Sartre, her companion, women had been philosophically invisible as a question. Moreover, there had been no great women philosophers throughout that two and a half millennia of philosophical debate. Thus, for many ordinary men and women in classical Greece, the gods and goddesses were as important as they were for the Egyptians and other societies.

Furthermore, although it is often pointed out that polytheistic interpretations of eternal reality often portray gods and goddesses as immoral and unworthy of respect and devotion, the lives and deeds of some philosophers do not bear overmuch scrutiny. Pythagoras (571–496 BCE) drowned one of his students, Hipparsus of Tarentum, for revealing to outsiders that the world is not quite mathematically explicable. Although the oracle at Delphi called the great Socrates (470–399 BCE) the 'wisest man in Greece', it overlooked his political ineptitude. He was friendly to some of the 'Thirty Tyrants' who executed many of their Athenian opponents. It was for that reason, as much as for his supposed corruption of young men by his ideas, that he was condemned to death.

More important, it is necessary to ask the right questions about a polytheistic view of reality. It is quite true that the stories of deities in Egypt, Greece, Rome, Scandinavia, Germany and many other places do not wholly accord with contemporary notions about the good life. It is also true that, even in the ancient world, some Greeks and Romans condemned the stories of the gods and goddesses as unsuitable models for the truly human life. Yet that is to miss the fact, as we have seen in contemplating the story of Isis, Osiris, Seth and Horus, that they speak on several levels to the human experience of those who told and heard them. Only to focus on the perceived wrongdoings of the gods and goddesses is to miss the point, and also the humour and the pathos, of the tales.

Indeed, the widespread interest in aspects of this Egyptian story in ancient Greece and Rome, and its assimilation to the needs of different sorts of people there, shows how aspects of the tale transcend cultural and historical limitations. The Austrian composer Mozart's last opera, *The Magic Flute*, finished just before his death in 1791 CE, refracts aspects of the story of Isis and Osiris through various concerns of his life and times, including Masonic ritual! Another example of religious linkages between different times and places can be illustrated from words for gods in different societies. For example, the Greek Zeus is related to Sanskrit Dyaus and Saxon Tyw. One can make too much of this (as did the great Max Müller, who assumed that India was the original home of religion from where it spread further afield) but one can also make too little. Contemporary scholars who make much of the growing inter-connectedness of the world often forget that, even in ancient times, human beings did not live totally isolated from each other's worldviews.

A polytheistic vision of reality locates power and functions in a variety of deities. Even though, within a pantheon, one deity may stand out as particularly authoritative (as once were Zeus in Greece, and Odin in Sweden, Denmark, north Germany and England) rarely if ever does he or she exercise unlimited power. It is too glib an interpretation to assume that this reflects the rather primitive societies of their origin. Many such societies were far from primitive; though in times and places where many people rarely moved out of their village, they may have had little sense of a fundamental and greater unity beyond the horizon of their lives. It may seem the case, from other perspectives, that a polytheistic interpretation of ultimate reality locates power in too many foci of belief. Yet it is not an unworthy view of reality to assume that Transcendence bubbles up in the phenomenal world in many ways and forms. In some societies where a god or goddess gains widespread allegiance, this may reflect an instinct towards a unity within diversity. Moreover, monotheistic and other views of reality that emphasise the unity of life, this world and another plane of reality, have their own problems that may be corrected, or at least put in perspective, by comparing them with polytheistic visions. We shall return to this issue in the next section of this chapter.

Readers who live within a worldview that assumes that God, whether he is believed in or not, is necessarily depicted as all-powerful and in control of the course of events, may find it difficult to appreciate the assumptions of a polytheistic vision. We shall see in due course that the Buddha did not deny the existence of the gods, but certainly held that they cannot liberate individual people. His was merely an extreme example of the conviction in many societies that the deities perform certain functions but not others. Because Thor, the Scandinavian storm god, controlled lightning, was physically the strongest of the gods and a god of fertility, his devotees made offerings to him in those capacities, either to appease him or entreat him for a boon. They did not think of him as all-controlling.

Indian views of reality have a polytheistic component that is challenged by many Western views of how things should be. It is not uncommon to hear Indians claim that the numerous deities in popular religion are merely temporal expressions of the one God or else of the one enduring reality beyond all deities. True, such points of view have a long and distinguished pedigree in Indian history. Sometimes, however, contemporary Hindu proponents of this position seem to be making concessions to explicit or implicit yet very questionable Western notions of what should constitute a proper religion. India has many, often apparently contradictory, views of ultimate reality that exist cheek by jowl. It is often more interesting and informative to recognise that diversity than to explain it away, or reduce it to the preferred wisdom of an individual or particular group.

In at least two respects, Indian views of polytheism challenge certain Western notions of the inadequacies of a polytheistic system. First, in India, philosophical discourse has co-existed with a polytheistic system, as it did in ancient Greece. Yet many Indian philosophers have been more accepting of the gods and goddesses than were some ancient Greek men. Many, however, have interpreted the gods, who exist in this phenomenal world, as ultimately transient rather than eternal. However, that does not take away from the gods the roles that they can perform for their devotees within this mundane existence. Second, devotion to one god or aspect or down-coming (*avatara*) of a god can be transformative of human life. It is difficult for contemporary humans to understand, without a great effort of imagination, the depth of devotion that an ancient Egyptian gave to her god, which changed her life for good. However, it is possible nowadays to see the effect that Krishna devotion has upon Hindus who engage in it.

We may conclude that a polytheistic interpretation of reality is attractive to many people in society; not just to those who love stories but especially to those who engage with the stories so that they see in them a means of understanding the world around and even beyond. This engagement is rarely expressed in an intellectual way. Rather, people express their commitment by telling and retelling the stories, and in acts of devotion to the gods and goddesses.

monotheism

The French Egyptologist, Christian Jacq, has recently turned his hand to a series of popular novels about Pharaoh Ramses II, who ruled Egypt for sixty-seven years from 1279 to 1212 BCE. In them, one of Ramses's childhood friends is Moses who, as the novels have it, comes under the dark influence of a supporter of the dead pharaoh, Akhenaten. Ramses lets him leave Egypt with the Hebrews. Some scholars (e.g. Assmann, 1998, *passim*) have believed that Akhenaten had a direct impact upon the religion of the Hebrew leader, Moses, whose name is Egyptian, meaning 'saved from water' (as indeed he was, according to Exodus 2:10). Certainly, the pharaoh's hymn to the Aten is similar to the form and sentiments of later Hebrew psalms (its conceptions are very close to those of Psalm 104). If his religion did influence that of Moses, then Jewish, Christian and arguably Islamic monotheism derives from this remarkable figure of the eighteenth Egyptian dynasty. It is fascinating to speculate that Jewish monotheism was indebted to the vision of an accursed pharaoh. However, that is all one can do. There is no proof, only supposition. It is certainly true that the Jews were chiefly responsible for introducing the belief in one God into history and the human imagination.

The historical Moses is a shadowy figure, as of course are most people from the ancient world. If there is truth in the stories of the exodus of the Jews from Egypt under his leadership, which the balance of probability supports, that event could well have taken place under Ramses II or his successor. The Hebrews' journey to Palestine took an impossibly long forty years, well past the life-span of most people then, suggesting that only a new generation of Jews would actually inherit God's promises. Their God made a covenant with them on Mount Sinai; he gave Moses two tablets of stone on which the Ten Commandments were written. (The exact location of this mountain is unknown though Christians have identified it with Jebel Musa near to the monastery of St Catherine in southern Sinai.) When Moses came down from the mountain with them, he discovered his people worshipping the golden calf. In a fit of anger he cast the tablets from his hands and broke them (Exodus 32:19). He pleaded with God to forgive the people. God relented and Moses was told to fashion two new tablets on which God would again write the commandments (Exodus 34:1).

This story would be incomprehensible in many polytheistic societies: why should people not worship one god whilst their leader was doing business with another one? Scholars of the Hebrew Bible often point out that the Jews were committed to an ethical monotheism. True, this story is about Ten Commandments and (in later Jewish development of the story) the beginning of written and oral law that has governed Jewish belief and especially practices ever since. This ethical component quite probably distinguishes Jewish monotheism from the interpretation of Akhenaten. The Aten gave life to the world each day as it blazed across the sky, but it does not seem to have made any profoundly moral demands on Egyptians; though we may simply know too little about the pharaoh's religious experiment to be sure of this.

The Hebrew Bible contains much old material but it was compiled later in the first millennium BCE by people who had come to a rather fixed view that God was one and that he made ethical and other demands upon his people. It is possible for contemporary readers to discern that this view was the result of a process during which things were much less clear-cut. The story of the worship of the golden calf shows that monotheism is not the natural religion of the world that many people believe it to be. (It is a popular conviction among Muslims that babies are born Muslim, submitters to the one God, and are led into other beliefs by their parents, but there is not much evidence from the history of religions for this pious belief.) It could be that Moses' people were disobedient, as scripture emphasises. It could be nearer the mark that they had to be educated into the new ways of believing and behaving. Probably they could not comprehend why there should be one God rather than many. Indeed, there are indications that this one God was not one in the sense that his existence intended and insisted upon the denial of the reality of others. Rather, he was the god of the Jews, whom they must obey and serve to the exclusion of others. Later this belief developed into a stricter form of monotheism, making him the only God. There are many stories in the Bible indicating that some Jews could never bring themselves to believe and obey the insight that their God was a jealous God who brooked no rivals, not just in the days of Moses but for centuries thereafter.

It was probably the vicissitudes and tragedies that the Jews faced that developed their belief that only their God was effective. Their territory was surrounded by greater powers: the Egyptians, Assyrians, Babylonians and Persians. Hence, there was always the likelihood that they would be vassals of other empires. In 722 BCE, the Northern Kingdom fell to the Assyrians, and ten of the twelve tribes disappeared from history. After the first Temple in Jerusalem was destroyed by the Babylonians in 586 BCE, many Jews were exiled to Babylon. From then onwards, many Jews lived in the Diaspora (the 'dispersion' among the nations). After the Jewish war against Rome when the second Temple was destroyed in 70 CE, and the Bar Kochba rebellion that ended in 135 CE, Jews finally lost any realistic hope of controlling their holy land until the creation of the state of Israel in 1948 CE (though there have been Jews in Palestine throughout that period).

If they had operated within a polytheistic vision, the Jews would no doubt have come to the conclusion that their God, whom they revered so much that they refused to name him directly but only in circumlocutory form, was rather a powerless figure. Indeed, some did reach the conclusion that he was impotent before more powerful gods, but many others did not. Instead, members of this latter group explained what happened in terms of Israel's covenant relationship with God. They deduced that God had punished his people for their sins, though most held that he would never utterly abandon them. The eighth-century BCE prophet Amos expressed this in a forceful way: 'You only have I known of all the families of the earth; therefore I will punish you for all your iniquities' (Amos 3:2). This point of view enabled Jews to continue to believe in God's control of human events, and also emphasised the need for the people to avoid lusting after false gods and to follow an ethic of social justice. The unknown prophet of the Babylonian exile, whose words are contained in Isaiah chapters 40 to 55, confidently proclaimed the majesty and power of God at a time when Jews could be forgiven for thinking that he was puny and unable to stand up to Bel and Marduk, and other deities of the victorious Babylonian and Persian empires. Ironically, the Jews' experiences of abandonment by their God led to a growing sense that he was not simply the god of the Jews, or the most important of all the gods, but was in fact the only God.

Nowadays, Jews are deeply committed to the conviction that God is one. So, also, are Muslims. Jews recite the *Shema* based on Deuteronomy chapter 6 verse 4: 'Hear, O Israel, the Lord our God, the Lord is One.' Muslims, too, emphasise the unity of God. They recite the *Shahada*: 'I bear witness that God alone is God, and that Muhammad is his Prophet.' Zoroastrians (called Parsees in contemporary India), many Hindus and Christians are also monotheists; but more eccentrically or at least unusually so. The prophet Zoroaster, whose dates are often given as 628–551 BCE, was called by the supreme God, Ahura Mazda, to preach a message of monotheism in Eastern Persia. As the religion developed, the old gods became transformed into different classes of spiritual beings. Because devotees believed that evil could not come from God, it was imputed to an opposing principle of darkness and lies, Ahriman, whom Ahura Mazda will eventually overcome. Thus, though monotheism ultimately prevails, some have deemed Zoroastrianism a dualistic religion. (We shall examine Hinduism in the next section of this chapter.)

Christian Trinitarianism is enshrined in the creeds of the fourth century, though deep reverence for Jesus and the Spirit of God is firmly located in the witness of the New Testament. Some outsiders, and even a few Christians themselves, have asserted that the apostle Paul subverted the simple message of Jesus by applying to it speculative Greek thought and that the fathers of the church of the early Christian centuries developed this with pedantic literalness. On this view the notion of God as Trinity is an unnecessary and misleading elaboration. Yet this is not a credible argument, not least because Jesus' message was itself more subversive and less simple than many have held or hoped. It may well be the case that if the Christian revelation had occurred in the twentieth century, devotees would have found a different cultural garb to clothe the truths at which the doctrine of the Trinity aims. But it seems likely that they would have been forced by the evidence to deal with the same issue: that the man Jesus was linked with the creator God and the indwelling Spirit of God in the process of human (and even cosmic) transformation. This doctrine has two important emphases. First, there is the work of God in bringing about that process of transformation, through the life, death and resurrection of Jesus and the gift of the Spirit at Pentecost. Secondly, there is the insight it gives into God's inner life of divine love that outpours itself upon humankind and enables such a transformative process.

From Jewish and Muslim perspectives, the Christian doctrine of the Trinity seems an eccentric, even aberrant kind of monotheism. Yet this criticism is not necessarily as convincing as it may first seem. In the Vedic scriptures of Hinduism, various gods are associated with the Trimurti, 'three formed', but in the epic Mahabharata the three are mainly Brahma, Vishnu and Shiva. Mahayana Buddhism has a notion of Trikaya, 'three bodies', according to which the Buddha appeared in different 'bodies' to distinct groups. Furthermore, as Taoism developed in China, its teachers worshipped a Triad of heavenly gods: the Grand Unity, Heavenly Unity and Earthly Unity. Of course, there are great differences between these 'triune' beliefs in the various religions of the world. Yet the insight that the nature of God is relational (the second of the insights of Christian Trinitarian belief) was uncovered by religions of India long before it occurred to the Western religious imagination. Characteristically, Indian religious experience developed this into an exuberant profligacy, so that there have been many manifestations of the divine nature. This belief, at least in Hinduism and Christianity and arguably elsewhere, of a Transcendent grace and goodness whose self-giving love overflows within the created order of this world and universe, has immense consequences for the devotional and ethical lives of devotees, as we shall see in later chapters.

Fascinatingly, there are hints within both Judaism and Islam that the unity of God was not as watertight or 'boundaried' as it might seem. Particularly during and after the exile to Babylon, Jewish faith was deeply influenced by ethical and proverbial maxims of the 'wise' that circulated widely in West Asia and Egypt. Characteristically, Jews conformed this to a monotheistic vision: 'The fear of the Lord, that is wisdom; and to depart from evil is understanding' (Job 28:28). In the process, wisdom was eventually declared to be the beginning of God's works (Proverbs 8:22). These and similar passages, led to speculation about wisdom as God's spokesperson on earth and thereafter to a tradition about Lady Wisdom. She makes her home on earth and invites to her all who seek life. In the deuterocanonical wisdom literature she opts to reside in Israel, at Jerusalem, and takes the form of the Law of Moses. She becomes an expression of divine personality, overflowing to certain people. One of these, King Solomon, she marries. It would be misleading to suggest that in mainstream Judaism wisdom and God are coterminous, so that wisdom is God alongside God; though early Christian writers, Matthew, John and Paul, implicitly or explicitly developed the belief that Jesus was the wisdom of God, alongside God. Nevertheless, there is the sense in Jewish convictions about wisdom that the one God has a variety of means of manifesting herself in this mundane existence. (Wisdom is feminine in form in both Hebrew and Greek.)

The genius of Islam has been to enshrine the quranic ideal of a single human community in which political, social and economic matters are held together as the will of the one God for humankind. Yet there are indications that, early in his prophetic career, Muhammad was tempted to compromise the absolute unity of God by, at the very least, allowing Meccan goddesses to function as intercessors with God (Forward, 1997, pp.34–36).

The advantages of belief in one God seem obvious to cultures in which such a belief has taken deep root. Devotees of a monotheistic vision can point to the fact that this interpretation of Transcendent reality emphasises a unity and consistency of Transcendent being, will, purpose and power. A variety of gods and goddesses can kill each other or work to accomplish different ends for themselves and their worshippers! Not so when one God works to accomplish his or her purpose.

Yet the ambivalence of the pronoun in that sentence indicates certain problems with the concept of one God, which we shall develop in the course of this book. Certainly, proponents of God's unity have often pictured the deity in strongly anthropomorphic terms. God is often depicted as masculine, and as a jealous God who is quick to punish those who stand in the way of his purpose. Only in the contemporary world have people begun to raise questions about the oppression of women by patriarchal language and structures of power. Members of monotheistic religions have not always pictured the one God as God of the one world, but have been content to domesticate the deity within their own tradition of faith; sometimes even within one branch of that faith to the exclusion of others. In the contemporary world, a monotheistic vision needs to be a universal vision, embracing all of humankind as children of God.

Of course, the deepest teachings of the great monotheistic religions have not supported a popular view of God as an all-powerful superhuman man, with a tendency to violence, who is surprisingly easily manipulated by self-appointed true believers. Rather, God is eternal spirit, the vastness of being beyond our sight and, in all God's fullness, beyond even our mind's eye to know and to celebrate. Precisely because our knowledge of God is partial, unpacking this mystery leads to important differences even within religions. For instance: does God possess to the nth degree the world's perfections, or is (s)he completely other?

The apparent remnants of a polytheistic outlook within strongly monotheistic religions like Islam and Judaism could simply indicate earlier elements within the traditions that are now superseded. But evidence from Zoroastrianism and Christianity indicates that God in monotheistic belief is not as univocally one as some hold. Within the overarching recognition that Transcendence has a unity of being, thought and purpose, many monotheistic religions make space for diversity, subtlety and mystery. Perhaps modern

psychology can help us here. This discipline enables individual
humans to see themselves as complex, multifaceted and mysterious.
Even so, each individual, however complicated and many-sided she
is, remains clearly one person. So it may be with the nature and
being of Transcendent reality.

the one and the many

It is perhaps Indian religion that has most clearly given expression
to a sense of unity and diversity within religious life. To its insights,
and then to other insights from China and Africa, we now turn.

India is irredeemably pluralistic, with many languages, many
'schools' of Hindu faith, and with great social diversity in the caste
system. For the Hindu, the nature of Transcendence is a kind of
divine lavishness, overflowing in myriad forms in this world. In
certain Hindu traditions, Transcendence is encountered in either
sex or even both sexes, sometimes animal in form, exuberantly
playful and diverse. Like Christians, many Hindus believe that
Transcendence is multifaceted, but do not restrict its manifestations
to three but to thousands, even millions of forms.

Fundamental to an understanding of Hinduism is the concept of
Brahman. This is the supreme soul of the universe, the Absolute in
Hindu philosophy. (Indian religion has never separated philosophy
and theology as have, for example, Christianity and Islam.)
Brahman derives, perhaps, from a root *brih*, meaning 'to roar'. In the
Upanishads, the oldest of which date from about 800 to 300 BCE,
Brahman sustains the earth, pervades the universe and, indeed, is
present everywhere. In the Upanishads, Atman (deriving from a
word meaning 'breath' and sometimes denoting the individual soul,
but at others the soul of the universe) is often another name for
Brahman. Brahman is indescribable; it can only be described as
'*neti, neti*', 'not this, not that'.

Many scholars, such as Geoffrey Parrinder (1997, first published
in 1970), have argued that there are both monistic and theistic
traditions in India. Monism, which comes from the Greek *monos*,
meaning 'one', is the belief that only one being exists. This,
Parrinder, believes, is the natural if somewhat austere way to
understand Brahman. We are all caught up as part of the great

oneness of being that is essentially impersonal. Yet Parrinder
believes that most humans cannot live with such an intangible and
subtle conception, so there co-existed a strongly theistic view. In his
opinion, the famous Bhagavad Gita, written towards the beginning
of (perhaps just before) the Common Era, returns to a theistic
vision of reality. In it, the god Krishna, who is on earth as the
charioteer of Arjuna, appears in his true, godlike form. However, a
number of Hindu philosophers have not read the Bhagavad Gita in
a theistic way. So perhaps we are best recognising that the Hindu
scriptures, traditions and philosophical reflections point in a
number of directions, and enable Hindus to develop their religious
past in fruitfully different ways.

In fact, the distinction between theism and monism, though
once widely held and a useful distinction, may be too clear cut to
reflect the many ways Hindu religious expressions describe the
manifestations of the one and the many (see Lipner's article in
Forward, 1995, pp.167–175). Monism emphasises that ultimate
reality is not simply *behind* this mundane existence, but *within* it, so
that all things are suffused with the eternal now.

Furthermore, the assumption that Brahman is essentially neuter
and impersonal is overstated. Hindu and other forms of Indian faith
have affirmed that Transcendence is beyond our notions of gender
and not to be mistaken for an old man in the sky. Thus Hinduism
has often avoided the delusion common in certain popular forms
of, for example, Christianity and Islam that God is a powerful man.
Yet although Brahman is ultimately beyond human capacity to
describe in words, it engages with this world (or perhaps a better
image is that it operates within it) in powerfully various ways.
Characteristically, the one becomes the many. In certain religions,
monotheism is often viewed as a development and replacement of
polytheistic belief, though we have seen reasons to question aspects
of this judgement. In Hinduism, the many gods are an outpouring
of the great void that lies beyond this world.

Yet in some South Asian forms of religious beliefs, the gods are
not ultimately part of human deliverance from this world's joys and
troubles. Arising out of Hinduism, Buddhism accepts the idea of
many births and a cyclical view of history. Indeed, it is crucial to an
understanding of the Buddha's teaching. This can be illustrated
from the night of his enlightenment or awakening. In the first watch

of the night, he remembered his previous lives within *samsara* (rebirth), the never ceasing wheel of life. In the second watch, he understood that people's present experiences were caused by *karma*, their previous actions. In the Buddhist view of things, the gods, too, are caught up on the wheel of *samsara*. They are not able to liberate people. Each individual (and each god) has to work out her own *nirvana* (or escape from *samsara* into the freedom of never being born again). We shall look at certain of these concepts again. The point at present is to illustrate this idea that gods are not always viewed as ultimately powerful. In Egypt, Greece and elsewhere, this is often because they perform specific roles alongside other deities. Aspects of this are found in Buddhism. Many Buddhists go to particular deities for help in certain particular matters, but they are not envisaged as all-powerful, ultimately liberative agents. This Buddhist attitude towards the gods also resonates with some teaching in the Hebrew Bible where they are not so much denied as reduced to relatively impotent roles, either minor deities or members of the angelic host. Maybe Muhammad's initial willingness to accept Meccan goddesses as intercessors between humans and the one God also picks up the same impetus to reduce the role of the gods to a secondary or even marginal position.

In China, religion has been deeply influenced by Indian faith, especially by Buddhism, which spread there from about the beginning of the Common Era. In turn, it greatly influenced Japanese traditions of faith. It is a fallacy to claim, as many do, that religion has played an insignificant role in Chinese life and culture. True, it has differed from Western religion in that institutionalised religion has been rather weak; but that is changing in the West now; and many other non-Western cultures do not emphasise the institutional dimension of religion as important. Confucianism, Taoism and Buddhism have been of particular importance in China, but it has also embraced Nestorian Christianity and Islam, and has even flirted with the secular ideology of Maoism.

Yet as early as the later stages of the Shang dynasty (*c.*1760 to *c.*1122 BCE), the most characteristic features of a Chinese religious worldview were in place. They centred on: a cult of ancestors revered in a highly organised ritual; the connection of religion with the state, which flowed from the notion that those in authority performed religious functions whilst others observed them; a great emphasis upon the correct and meticulous observance of ceremonial; and the conviction that the main concern of religion was to establish a harmonious relationship between heaven, earth and humans.

How was 'heaven' depicted? Since this early period, Chinese people have believed in a Supreme Being who presides over a hierarchy in the spiritual world that was closely entwined with human life and destiny. In Shang times, that being was known as Ti. The Chou successors to the Shang dynasty turned the Supreme Being from a primeval ancestor spirit to High God, calling it Shang Ti or Tien. Ti had been the founder of the Shang dynasty. In his new guise, he was presented as one who demanded righteousness and orderly government, and withdrew his favour in their absence. Thus began the concept of the Mandate (*ming*) of Heaven, which rulers received from Tien who could withdraw it if necessary. By this means the Chou rulers justified their rebellion against the Shang dynasty, but also paved the way for their own overthrow in the fifth century BCE. Nevertheless, the Chou reinterpretation of Transcendence replaced a polytheistic system with a clear concept of a High God, who controlled Heaven, and made ethical demands of rulers as well as their subjects. Other heavenly beings exist, but in a strictly subordinate role. Writings in Chou times speak of the ancestors of the Chou clans, kings Wen and Wu, and even of the god of millet, Hou Chi, the clan deity, as 'associated with' Tien, not as his equal. Deceased ancestors were associated with the Supreme God but not identified with him.

In traditional African faith, there are also similar emphases. At the end of the 1940s, Geoffrey Parrinder proposed a fourfold classification of West African traditional religion: a Supreme God, chief divinities, the cult of the human but divinised ancestors, and charms and amulets. Over the next few years, he added to this categorisation the African conviction that a life force exists in all things, and he extended his interpretation to include not just West Africa but the whole of the continent south of the Sahara Desert. Other scholars have developed this fourfold model. African Christians have emphasised the concept of the Supreme God in African faith. They have been heavily criticised by anthropologists and others for 'creating' an African God based on a foreign Christian template; justly, to some extent. Yet the critics are also to be criticised. It is certainly the case that most African groups do have a notion of a Supreme God, even if it is not always as easily matched to Christian views of God as many African Christian scholars have asserted. Moreover, even some contemporary anthropologists miss the wood for the trees: a wider knowledge of religious experience, especially in South Asia and China, would assist some to see that there does seem to be a universal human impetus towards the one and the many. In other words, concepts of a Supreme Being are found in many human communities, including many that, at least until recently, have been isolated from and ignorant of each other. Further, they often do exist within either a polytheistic system or a monotheistic system where the concept of unity does not preclude a measure of diversity (Forward, 1998a, pp.73–97).

tribal or universal?

It is easy to mock the claim that all religious experience is good and acceptable. The Aztecs who held up the still-beating hearts of their victims to the sun do not seem to be in touch with the same universal reality as St Francis of Assisi and Mahatma Gandhi (or perhaps it is better to suggest that they do not seem to have understood its demands as well as the aforementioned individuals). Yet the fact that people misunderstand, even seriously and tragically, the demands and even the nature of ultimate reality does not necessarily mean that the same reality is not impinging upon their hearts and minds as it is upon others'.

This leads to the important question: if there is a common human impulse towards the one and the many, is there also a sense that all the claimed manifestations of Transcendence in the arena of this life are to be affirmed? In other words, are all religions responses to the truth? Not so, claim many adherents of the world's religions; though it is interesting to observe that such people rarely if ever believe that the religion in which they have been reared is the wrong one and another is the true faith.

For much of Christian history, missionaries have spread the gospel or good news of Jesus on the grounds that it is better news than others had previously heard. Islam and Buddhism are also great missionary religions. In the modern world, members of religions that have not traditionally been strongly mission-conscious, Hindus in particular, have also sought and made converts. Fundamentalist or at least deeply conservative interpretations of many religions are making greater headway than more liberal and open constructions. Clearly, some of these exclusive convictions arise out of paranoia, prejudice, or a desire for false security and certainties in a fast-changing world.

Even so, many religions began because of certain definite differences with their host-faith. Buddhism and Jainism arose as reform movements within Indian religion as, to some extent, did Christianity within a Jewish and Gentile matrix. Attempts to ignore these differences are as futile as are endeavours to overestimate them. Certainly, the facile assumption or assertion that all religions are paths up the same mountain will not do: who is the superior person who can see all other humans struggling to get to the summit that she herself has reached?

Indeed, the universal claims of many inclusive interpretations of religion are often, ironically, rather superior in tone. In chapter 1, we noted that, despite the great learning of many proponents of the perennial philosophy, they never really argue their case but just assume that it is self-evidently true that imperishable wisdom bubbles up in all faiths. The interpretation of Hinduism that includes Jainism, Buddhism and even Sikhism within the Hindu family of faiths, without recourse to the views of Jains, Buddhists and Sikhs, may intend friendship and inclusiveness but can be received as impertinence and ignorance. There are similar, inclusive views, in most other faiths.

Ironically, pluralists are just as guilty of conforming others to their own view of reality. Pluralists are those who believe that all religions are potentially liberative and transformative vehicles for believers, and do not intentionally conform religions to a single perspective. Yet in practice most do. John Hick is probably the most distinguished contemporary proponent of pluralism. His vision of pluralism looks suspiciously like the universalisation of certain aspects of Western philosophy (particularly Kant) and of liberal Protestantism (Hick, 1995, *passim*; Forward, 1998b, pp.149–160).

There is, of course, great variety between religions: for example, the Christian belief in the God and Father of the Lord Jesus Christ looks very different indeed from a Buddhist concept of the void. Even within religions, there is enormous diversity. Muslims have always emphasised the unity and integrity of their religion, which mirrors the unity of God. Yet a tradition has the Prophet Muhammad say that his people will divide into seventy-three sects, all of which except for one will go to hell. That looks suspiciously like a later reflection on the divergences of belief and practice within early Islam (probably by those who deemed themselves within the one, correct but exclusive, sect). Indeed, Islam has many and varied religious and cultural practices. Although Sunni Islam's proponents have often asserted its orthopraxy (the fact that its practices are normative for Muslims), that interpretation of Islam is a varied phenomenon itself, and has not gained the allegiance of all Muslims. Indeed, internal variety, often leading to much bickering and even anathematising, is a feature of all world religions.

It is helpful to focus the issue in a different way. Let us grant that religions are multifaceted phenomena and often offer very different, seemingly irreconcilable, interpretations of fundamental matters of living and dying, both from other religions and even from variant expressions of the same faith. Indeed, let us illustrate this point, and, in the process, cast light on the further matter that different religious expressions (often intrafaith as well as interfaith) can meet different needs or open up new opportunities for marginalised or disregarded groups.

Buddhism grew out of Hindu expressions of faith. The story of Prince Siddhartha's early life illustrates what he was in reaction against. As a youngster, he was protected from the transience of life, its impermanence, suffering and decay. Then, around his thirtieth year, when a husband and father, he left the palace with only his charioteer. He saw an old man, a sick man, a corpse and a meditating monk. He was plunged into mental turmoil, and decided to leave home and family. It was compassion that compelled him to renounce all he held dear. He attempted to discern what would overcome illness, old age and death. He tried meditation and asceticism before, under a Bo tree, he woke up to life's deepest meaning, to the middle way that would liberate humankind from that attachment to the self that causes pain, suffering and loss. Thus he became the Buddha, the enlightened or awakened one.

So the Buddha reacted against aspects of the Hinduism of his day: against the developing caste system, against meditative practices that did not work and excessive mortification of the flesh.

A figure cut in stone representing the Buddha seated under the Bo tree with his right hand in the Abhaya mudra (gesture of fearlessness), which he adopted immediately after his enlightenment.

He implied that the religion of the day had no helpful solution to the impermanence of life. Yet much bound him to that system: we have seen that he accepted current concepts such as *samsara* and *karma*. His may have been a radical reformation, but it was the re-formation of a tradition and not its abandonment. Even if a new religion grew up that broke the boundaries of Indian-ness as it moved in East Asia, it was nevertheless profoundly indebted to its past.

Much recent work on Jewish–Christian Relations in a post-holocaust world has stressed the indebtedness of Christianity to its Jewish roots. Despite the heated debates between Jesus and some of his contemporaries, more bound them together than divided them: including the belief in an ethical monotheism and the conviction that God had given Torah to Moses as part of his covenantal relationship with Jews. Some scholars have argued that Paul over-complicated the simple message of Jesus with Greek philosophical concepts. Rather, he grounded Jesus' version of Jewish faith in a cultural garb that enabled it to spread among Gentiles. In doing so, early Christianity built upon one strand of Jewish teaching. In fact, it was the dispersal of Jews amongst polytheistic communities in the ancient world that enabled some pagans to hear and be gripped by a message of the one God. Paul himself grew up in Tarsus, on the road leading from Asia Minor to Syria. He was eminently fitted to universalise the Jewish message, in the sense of interpreting it in ways that helped it to spread within the cultural matrix of the first century CE Mediterranean world.

It is not too fanciful to speculate that Christianity did for Jewish faith what Buddhism did for Hindu faith: they effected transformations upon the matrix of beliefs from which they sprang that enabled them to spread more easily from the regions of their birth to far-flung lands. That does not mean of course that they were necessarily better religions; only that they took up a form or forms that enabled them to acquire a more universal acceptance. Of course, this came at a price. That cost included alienation from the religious matrix from which they sprang, and the development of beliefs and practices that other religious expressions within that matrix would deem inauthentic. Yet even this cost can be overstated. Indian (and also Chinese) religious expressions have usually been remarkably accommodating to the reform movements that have sprung up on their soil, and even to outside faiths of Christianity and Islam that have gained footholds there.

In the process of this religious re-formation and development, it was not just Buddhism and Christianity that were re-formed. Hinduism was greatly reshaped around the end of the first millennium CE by the teachings of great figures like Shankara and Ramanuja. Its renewal led to the almost complete removal of Buddhism from the land of its birth. After the war with Rome and the destruction of the Second Temple in 70 CE, Judaism, too, was transformed by the rabbis. It is best to regard Christianity and Judaism as different developments of Jewish faith in the first century of the Common Era, than to depict Judaism as the mother of Christianity.

Even faiths that have no missionary impetus often imply or even argue the case that the Transcendent reality whom they venerate is for all, available to others in appropriate ways. Judaism provides an example of this. The rabbis developed the concept that every non-Jew is a 'child of the covenant of Noah'. In theory, these Noahide laws are based on the commandments given to Adam and Noah. Since these two are ancestors of all humans, the obligations upon them fall upon all. These obligations usually include: the prohibition of idolatry, blasphemy, bloodshed, sexual sins, theft, eating from a live animal, and the command to establish a legal system. In more modern times, Jewish interpreters such as Franz Rosenzweig (1886–1929) in Europe and Abraham Heschel (1907–72) in America have argued that God honours the faith of others than Jews. Rosenzweig restricted true religion to Judaism and Christianity, believing Islam to be a parody of them. Heschel, rather, argues that it seems to be the case that God wills there to be more than one religion; the role of American Judaism is to reawaken the religious life of all America (Coward, 1985, pp. 7–9). Of course, some people break the Noahide commands, or even, in their ignorance, have no knowledge of them. But the point is that Jews have the resources to believe that God is available to all people everywhere, even though this does not deliver them from the responsibility of, in some measure, hearing his voice and responding to it.

Islam regards itself as the last and final religion, with Muhammad as the seal of the prophets (Quran 33:40). After he moved to Medina, Muhammad hoped that Jews and Christians would support him in his prophetic vocation. He was angered that this did not happen, and punished Jews in particular. Nevertheless, the Quran sees him as the reformer of a monotheism that dates back to Adam, the first man and prophet. Although there are exclusive verses in the Quran, which condemn non-Muslims, many Muslims quote with approval that which reads:

> Believers, Jews, Christians and Sabaeans [possibly the Mandaeans of Southern Iraq], whoever believes in God and the last day, and does what is right, will have a reward from their Lord (2:62).

Furthermore, most Muslims read the quranic references to Jews and Christians as 'people of the Book' in a positive light, though these references are partly hostile because they have misread and disobeyed their scriptures. When Islam later spread into Christian and Jewish areas, this concept encouraged Muslims to allow these and monotheistic groups to cleave to their faith, so long as they were submissive and paid a poll-tax, the *jizya*. Indeed, the Sufi (Islamic mystical) spread of Islam into India led some Muslim scholars to include Hindus (and their Veda) as people of the book (Coward, 1985, pp.55–58).

Muslims are nevertheless quite clear that they preserve the original monotheism, which other groups have sullied. They emphatically do not see Islam as a Johnny-come-lately religion. Indeed, it is the primal faith of humanity, which the Quran recovered for people to follow. Most faiths have a similar belief that they reveal what has always been the case. For example, the opening verses of John's Gospel establish Jesus as the incarnate word of God, who spoke at the beginning to bring forth creation and redemption (John 1:1–18). Thus, the incarnate word, Jesus of Nazareth, tells humans what God has always been like, not what he has been like since about 4 BCE to 30 CE. Many Hindus describe their faith as *sanatana dharma*, the eternal tradition or religion, whose origins lie beyond history in what Transcendence is always like.

The word 'tradition' is important for all religious people. The manifold expressions of the world's religions usually claim to unfold or give insight into the eternal, unchanging nature of ultimate reality and its claims upon all people everywhere. Few if any religions believe that they are inventing reality for the first time. Rather, they are depicting, on the human stage, a Transcendent reality that has always been as they claim it to be. Because many religions start as 'reform' movements, not *de novo*, any attempt at genuine novelty (rather than authentic development) in religion is bound to alarm a majority of those who have committed themselves to a way of life that focuses on the unchanging reality or realities that endure beyond this mundane and transient existence. Religions are conservative in the sense that they conserve what from the past has worked for individuals and societies. Even new religious movements usually claim some link with the past, whether real or spurious. Thus, for example, the Unification Church (commonly known as the Moonies because their human founder is the Reverend Moon) emphasises its roots in mainstream Christianity, and many New Age practitioners go back to gods and goddesses of Egypt and Mesopotamia to justify their beliefs and practices.

Another interesting contemporary phenomenon is the growing estimation and respect for ancestral religion held by many of the world's 'first people'. This is another example of the importance of past precedent and custom in religion. Aboriginal spirituality is now very important and is much studied and observed by small, though possibly growing, numbers of people. For the most part, such spirituality is not written but heard and transmitted from generation to generation by word of mouth. Who practice such traditional faiths? Some are indigenous people who live close to the land in America, Australia, Africa, certain Pacific islands and other places. Other practitioners are those of mixed ancestry who, unpersuaded by the claims of Christianity or secularism, choose the native religion of some of their ancestors. In Europe, a lively Neo-Pagan movement has sought to revive the ancient pre-Christian traditions. Such practitioners are enthusiasts who have no direct connection with those ways of faith.

Some religions have grown up specifically as attempts either to bring the different religions together, or else to contend that all are, in some measure, 'authorised' to mediate the Transcendent to humans. Let us briefly mention three.

Many Sikhs believe that, in origin, their religion began as an attempt to reform but also to reconcile Hindu and Muslim practices in the North Indian area of Punjab. Guru Nanak (1469–1539) was influenced by elements in both religions that emphasised mystical 'God-intoxication'. The Sikh scripture, the Adi Granth, was largely the creation of the fifth Guru, Arjan (d.1606) in 1603–1604, but it was added to until the tenth Guru Gobind Singh forbade further additions. It is unusual in that it contains not only the fifth Guru's compositions, but also verses of Hindu and Muslim holy people, including Kabir (d.1518), Namdev (d. c.1344) and Sheikh Farid (d.1265). True, the Christian faith 'borrowed' the Hebrew Scriptures as part of their own holy writ, but to some extent in a confrontational and fulfilment mode. The spirit behind Arjan's synthesis was quite different, even though the Muslim Emperor Jehangir martyred him. However, that martyrdom shows how difficult it is to blend and integrate different religious systems; too many people feel threatened by the process. Later Sikhism developed a much more militaristic and exclusive strand, in response to Muslim and then Hindu antagonism, though the earlier more peaceful and accommodating emphasis has never disappeared.

Baha'is are followers of Baha'u'llah, 'splendour of God', the title of Mirza Husain Ali (1817–92). He accepted the teaching of Ali Muhammad of Shiraz who, in 1822, declared himself the 'Bab' or 'gate' to divine truth. The Bab was charged with treason, and executed in 1850. In 1852, whilst exiled in Baghdad, Baha'u'llah declared he was the man whom the Bab had said God would manifest. The Baha'i faith teaches the unity of God, the truth of every religion, and continuous revelation in every age. Baha'u'llah taught that it would be wrong to prefer one prophet-founder of the world religions to another, since they come to different parts of the world and dress their message in the cultural garb they encounter. Further, the world is different now than it was, so the message of God changes in harmony with this difference. Even so, the basic message does not change: humans should love one another and seek peace. Again, Baha'i claims have caused dissent among the larger faith group of Shia Islam in Iran, so that recently Baha'is were seriously persecuted there.

The Unification Church was founded in Korea in 1954 by Sun Myung Moon. Its full title is the Holy Spirit Association for the Unification of World Christianity. In 1992, the Reverend Moon declared himself to be the Messiah who could accomplish what Jesus had failed to achieve: the establishment on earth of the Kingdom of God. The Unification Church hosts international conferences for religious scholars and eminent scientists. It has come in for much criticism, and even been linked to arms deals. Yet there is no need to doubt its strong impulse to bring the religions together in a common cause against atheistic communism but also, since the overthrow of that ideology in Europe, to pursue aims that unite the human race. Even the Reverend Moon's eccentric aim to build a road from East Asia through to Europe furthers that estimable aim. Like many New Religious Movements, the Unification Church has not had time to develop coherent aims, and has a bristly relationship with the mainstream religion from which it has evolved. Yet one can dimly perceive the intention to unite more than to divide, to offer the hope of a unity of religions and of science and religions, that has so far eluded the human race.

However, it does seem the case that humans enjoy diversity and are rarely convinced by attempts to establish a rigorous and totalitarian unity, even in their estimates of fundamental reality. It might be possible to regard this as an example of human fallibility or even sinfulness. It might just be the case, however, that this diversity somehow illustrates the nature of that reality itself (or himself, herself or even themselves!).

does it really matter whether anyone or anything is there?

Hindu mythology records the story that the God Shiva and the Goddess Parvati were playing around in their home in the Himalayan peaks when Parvati, in fun, covered Shiva's eyes with her hands. Thereupon the universe was engulfed in darkness. When Shiva's eyes are closed, light departs, except for the fire of his third eye which threatens destruction. The world's welfare depends upon the open eyes of the Lord.

This powerful image would make little sense to many people in the contemporary West, where God is ignored, forgotten or denied. The Protestant Christian reformer Martin Luther (1483–1546 CE) famously declared 'Let God be God', echoing sentiments expressed by many important men and women in religious history. This would mean listening to the demands of ultimate reality (however (s)he is named), and obeying them. Although nowadays many pay lip-service to the existence of a Transcendent dimension in life, they do not always seem to pay much attention to it; still less do they believe or even consider that it may require following with heart, soul, mind and spirit. Nor do they reflect on the possibility that the universe may, in the last resort, depend upon the goodwill, constant attention and care for it of that Transcendent dimension in life. To many people raised in a scientific and technological environment, the idea that God or Brahman, the Tao or the Void, may make sense of this visible world, qualitatively and actually, seems absurd. Yet religious people believe that, though science may explain how and even, to some extent, why things are as they are rather than otherwise, it merely offers the grammatical rules by which the language of life and death is uttered and interpreted. In their opinion, that language is also suffused with the Transcendent. Three interrelated questions should be asked of those who affirm that Transcendence matters.

First, is it possible that the same Transcendent reality lies behind all attempts to seek and be sought by it? My own view is that it is. Atheists would deny any such ultimate existence, and agnostics would claim to be unable to know of it. However, the myriad expressions of religious reality, however diverse, point to an alluring, demanding supreme reality. To that extent, the stories of Isis, Osiris, Seth and Horus brought Egyptian worshippers in contact with the same eternal reality as do Judaism, Taoism and other religious experiences in the contemporary world. Yet the story of Akhenaten returns to haunt and even rebuke those who would too easily interpret the religions of the world as basically in conformity with each other. Even within one universe of religious meaning there are many variant interpretations, often in competition with, or even antagonistic towards, each other. Even so, there remains the possibility that the same Transcendent reality lies behind all. Yet how we interpret that Transcendence for our contemporary world forces us to make choices that matter: not all responses to its demands are appropriate and life-giving.

The second is whether engagement with Transcendent reality provides a creative and relevant engagement with life. Aboriginal spirituality provides one example of how it does, or at least should do. For many first people, spirit permeates and animates matter. Religion is not an accessory to life, but held within a holistic view of living and dying. Nineteenth-century notions regarded first people as stuck at some primitive stage of development, a view still shamefully present in some circles today. Yet they are often reflective and deft partners of the natural world. Aboriginal teachings about human interaction with the environment are of importance to all who seek to mend the earth of human arrogance that has led to global warming and the like. Indigenous peoples have a respect for the earth and the life it supports, and a conviction that humanity is but one of many species who all have their place under the sun. These are the words of an Inuit (a member of a people who used to be called Eskimos): 'It is an important and special thing to be an Indian. Being an Indian means being able to understand and live with this world in a very special way. It means living with the land, with the animals, with the birds and fish as though they were your sisters and brothers. It means saying that the land is an old friend and an old friend your father knew, your people have always known... To the Indian people our land is really our life.' (quoted in Burger, 1990, p.16).

The third question is how do we contact that eternal reality, or how does it reach us? Hindu religious tradition records how important it is that the deities 'see' us, as the story of Shiva and Parvati illustrates. In the Hindu view, not only must the gods keep their eyes open but so must we, to see Transcendence, to receive its blessings and to penetrate its mysteries. If we lose the capacity to see, we shall suffer thereby. (We saw in chapter 1 how John Bowker has put this in modern garb, by suggesting that our genetically programmed capacity for being religious may atrophy if it is not used.) So we must turn to the subject of revelation in the world's religions: how we 'see' eternity and, much more importantly (so many religious people believe), how it 'sees' us.

how the transcendent sees us and we see the transcendent

Although the book of Job is found in the Hebrew Bible, Job himself is not described as a Jew. He is portrayed as a prosperous sheikh, with all that a man could hope for: material wealth, religious piety, a wife and family. Then calamity strikes him because God permits it. Job's sorrows come about in this way. God boasts to Satan of his blameless and upright servant, Job. Satan, whom we should interpret as an 'accuser' (which is what the word means in Hebrew) rather than a wicked devil, tells God that Job had every incentive to be blameless and upright, given the quantity of blessings he had received from the Almighty. But, Satan continues, if God were to reach out and take them away, Job would surely curse God to his face. God recoils from directly bringing misfortune upon Job, but tells Satan he can do what he likes; only, Satan must spare Job from the cataclysm. As a result, Job's prosperity is snatched away from him and his children die when a house falls on them. Nevertheless, Job takes it all and yet continues to worship God. God and Satan meet a second time. God cannot resist boasting to Satan about Job's enduring integrity. Satan says it would not survive Job's own physical misfortune, so God lets Satan have power over Job himself, except that he must not kill him. Poor Job is then afflicted with a serious skin complaint. His wife, understandably perhaps, tells him to curse God and die, but he refuses to do so, on the superhumanly heroic grounds that, if we accept good from God, we should also accept trouble.

Job's troubles get worse before they get better. He is afflicted with three friends who are keen that he should admit to some secret wrongdoing that would justify his misfortunes as deserved punishment. Later, another younger man joins the harangue, condemning the three 'comforters' but also finding equal fault with Job. Job himself maintains his innocence throughout, and appeals to God to vindicate him. Eventually God does so, appearing out of a whirlwind to show how much more he knows about the natural world than human beings, who ought therefore not to speak of what they do not know.

Aspects of the book of Job might trouble sensitive souls. God shuffles off responsibility for Job's misfortune by letting Satan afflict him. Thus the Almighty seems like a second-rate, shady politician who is only happy with power if it makes him popular and so turns over all the actions to some devious lackey who haunts the corridors of power for whatever small influence he might garner there. In the prose sections at the beginning and end of the book, Job is impressively long-suffering, inhumanly and even insufferably so. In the rest of the book, he is more inclined to expostulate and display anger and puzzlement. But in the prose section at the end, he once again becomes the wonderfully good man who prays for his tiresome and self-righteous friends and who is rewarded by increased prosperity, more sons and daughters, and ripe old age. Still, the reader wonders, are human relatives so easily replaced; is pain and anguish so readily healed?

It is very easy but misguided to treat the book with solemn literalness, looking for a consistency that is rarely found in the words and deeds of those who suffer greatly. Many scholars remind us that this work contains material from very different times and circumstances, which is not perfectly coherent. This is no doubt true, but someone or some group put it together, inconsistencies notwithstanding, to make it the book we now have. It is incredible to believe that they could not see the disjunctures that are so apparent to us. They seem to have permitted the seams to show, since that is how life is: seamy and unsatisfactory.

There is in fact a characteristically Jewish humour in this story, which points up the terrifying uncertainties in our mortal lives. God is both hidden and known; he is exactly like an all too predictable small town politician promoted above his competence, yet he is also the inscrutable governor of time and space. Job is a pious and righteous man of complete trust, exasperatingly so, but he is also angry and sometimes infuriatingly pious and even self-righteous. The friends mean well, but are also satisfied that catastrophes happened to someone else and not them, and, like so many self-appointed 'do-gooders', they indulge in the luxury of offering clichés in the guise of good advice. It is the nature of suffering to shake all our fixed certainties about who we are and what God is like. The shape of the book mirrors the inconsistencies of our own hopes and beliefs in the face of human pain and apparent divine contrariety.

Many issues resonate throughout this remarkable book. Perhaps the most desolate, yet also potentially empowering and hopeful, problem is: can humans readily trust God, who appears out of the impenetrable whirlwind; whom the unknown prophet of the second half of the book of Isaiah truly describes as a God who hides himself (45:15)? This question of the human capacity to know and be known by ultimate reality, however named, has universal resonance. Job speaks for many humans when he cries out: 'Oh that I knew where I might find him!' (23:3).

How, indeed, are humans to locate Transcendent reality? This issue of revelation lies at the heart of religion. At the close of chapter 2, we observed that some Hindus maintain that the universe exists because the all-seeing divine eye of the divine Lord holds it in view. They are not far from an insight of the book of Job, when God speaks out of the whirlwind and describes how he creates the universe and holds it in being. Both stories go on to emphasise the importance of the divine Lord's relationship with human beings: they imply not only that God sees us but that we must also attempt to see him.

In this chapter, we shall explore how human beings have believed that Transcendence sees them and they see it. So we shall examine: the world of art and aesthetics; holy places; holy word; and holy people. Afterwards, we shall examine the ways of mysticism, festivals and worship. These are paths which humans tread in order to reach out and respond to Transcendent revelation.

art and aesthetics

From the earliest moments of human history, art and aesthetics reveal the human obsession with ultimate reality. In chapter 1, we noted that tombs stained with ochre date back to Neanderthal times. Millennia later, the great pyramids at Giza, in the suburbs of modern Cairo, dating from about 2500 BCE, once contained the mummies of the Pharaohs Cheops and Khafre. They were no doubt far too easy targets for robbers, who soon after the pharaohs' deaths plundered their mummies and the artefacts that accompanied them on their trip through the world of the dead; so later pharaohs' tombs were buried underneath the sands of the desert. (The golden age of pyramid building, which began at Saqqara about 2780 BCE, came to an end at the conclusion of the sixth Dynasty in 2294 BCE.) Even so, very soon after the tombs of later pharaohs were constructed, many were looted by tomb-robbers, who were not daunted by the great attempts to keep their location secret. Visitors to the Egyptian museum in Cairo can see the contents of Tutankhamun's tomb, which survived ancient robbers (except for a minor incursion a few years after his death) only to be discovered in the 1920s by Lord Carnarvon and Howard Carter, whom some might call modern grave robbers. It is easy to be dazzled by the quantity, beauty and craftsmanship of the artefacts found in the tomb. Still, Tutankhamun was a very minor king, who died young in 1327 BCE. So it is likely that the tombs of the great pharaohs were even more impressive in size and in their contents.

If you move south from Cairo to the Valley of the Kings near Luxor (formerly Thebes), it is possible to visit such tombs, and see the remains of art and writing on the walls. Both the tombs themselves and their contents bear witness to human attempts to depict Transcendent realities in art and aesthetics. Of course, there were a number of reasons why pharaohs built their tombs. It was a display of their temporal power. Also, no doubt some of them were also inspired by beauty and the work of human hands, and took visceral enjoyment in the works they commissioned and often supervised. Yet the overarching reason was religious. Pharaohs came to embody the principle of *maat*: order and hierarchy. This political notion, even device, that legitimated the union of Upper and Lower

Egypt in the person of the pharaoh, also made him the focus of godly power. Into death, each ruler took goods as the symbol of that power. Yet as the climax of his journey after death, he was himself weighed in the balance to discern whether in life he had acted justly or not. The tombs and their contents illustrate the Egyptian belief that life on earth to some extent mirrored life in the world hereafter, a more comforting thought for kings and their wealthy courtiers perhaps than for the majority of Egyptians. Visitors to the remains of the contents of Tutankhamun's tomb, or to the graves of the pharaohs in the Valley of the Kings often, of course, go simply as tourists. But anyone who exercises their religious imagination, truly pondering what she sees, is surely struck by the hopes and beliefs of the ancient Egyptians that these remains illustrate: namely, that the mystery of life is mirrored by the mystery of the after-life.

So, from early days in the human story, art and aesthetics reveal a belief in a Transcendent dimension to life. Although writing was a feature of the tombs of the rulers of ancient Egypt, visitors are just as struck by the images there. The depictions of the deities, of the pharaoh himself, and of other functionaries and aspects of daily life are visually striking. Also remarkable is the pictorial nature of the hieroglyphs: the alphabet makes much use of birds, animals and human artefacts. This is surely natural in a society where the spoken word was more important than the written word for the vast majority of people. Even in today's world, reading is a skill unknown to a great number of people. So other senses, hearing, seeing and touching, are of great importance in stimulating the religious imagination.

Earlier generations of scholars of religion often thought that illiteracy was a sign of a primitive people with a quaint and rudimentary religion. Yet Geoffrey Parrinder has persuasively argued that this is not always or even usually the case. His career began in West Africa. He noted that Black African traditional religions have no scriptures. He put this fact down to the fact that Central and Southern Africa was isolated from literate societies by the Sahara desert and tropical forests. This may not be a sufficient explanation, but it is surely true as far as it goes.

Parrinder was frank about the problems of uncovering the heritage of the religions of illiterate people, not only in Africa but also in many other parts of the world. In an article published in honour of Mircea Eliade in 1971, he wrote that:

> Absence of religious literature meant that not only are there no written texts which transmit the thoughts of one generation to another, but there is no history of the religion and its development. It need not be doubted that there have been outstanding thinkers, priests, prophets, and poets, in Africa, America, and Australia. But they have disappeared with scarcely a trace, wasting their sweetness on the desert air. If they effected any changes in the direction of religious development, little or nothing is known of them... There is nothing from the inside, to tell us what it is like to belong to an illiterate religion. Reliance must be placed almost entirely on outside observation. (For this quotation and a summary of Parrinder's views, see Forward 1998a, pp.80–82)

That is where art and architecture come in, to give religious expression a tangible and lasting form. Parrinder's book *African Mythology* is a 'coffee-table' book with remarkable and suggestive photographs of African art and architecture. It has served to popularise his conviction that African art provides the purpose of a sacred literature. In it he contended that another source than art giving information about the essential nature of African ancestral religion is myth, stories passed down from generation to generation, collected first by Europeans and Americans who wrote down what Africans told them, and later by educated Africans. From these stories one can deduce African peoples' beliefs about the Supreme God, the Spirits, the ancestors and so on. Parrinder recounted many such stories about animals, describing, for example, how the leopard got its spots. The photographs of African art often illustrate and interpret the mythology. Meditation upon them helps outsiders to feel something of the attraction of ancestral faith for its adherents, and to assess it as a powerful, original and important religion of humankind.

Of course, one has to focus upon the object of the transmitted story in order for its meaning to become clear. One of the great storytellers was Jesus. His stories (known as parables) resonate in the imagination of those who listen and ponder. But, as he himself knew, not everybody gets the point. The parable of the sower tells of a man who went forth to sow. Some of his seed fell on the path and

(left) Ivory divining rod from the Yoruba of Nigeria, used in worship and fortune telling. (right) Wooden twin images from Abomey. Twin images are used in rituals to ensure the health of the twins, and if they die, the mother carries the images in her skirt band.

birds ate it up. Some fell on rocky places and sprang up but, because their roots had no depth, the shoots were scorched by the sun and withered. Some seed fell among thorns, which choked the growing plants before they could bear grain. Some seed fell on good soil and produced a crop (Mark 4:1–20). This may be a parable about parables, a story about stories. Many hear, but only some hear with an intuitive imagination that discerns in what it hears the alluring call of Transcendent grace and goodness, and acts upon what it hears. To use an expression that possibly derives from this parable, many hear and fall by the wayside.

Either you get the point of a story or you do not. Similarly, either you get the point of a religious image or you don't. From the 1500s onwards, Europeans in Africa and Asia observed local people bowing before or making some other reverent act to an image or images. Most were repelled by what they saw, and interpreted it as idolatry, worshipping bits of wood and stone, or other artefacts, instead of the one true God. In 1584, Ralph Fitch was the first

Englishman to visit Banaras, Hindu India's holiest city. He wrote
that:

> In this place, they be all Gentiles, and be the greatest idolaters that
> ever I sawe. To this towne come the Gentiles on pilgrimage out of
> farre countreyes. Here alongst the waters side bee many faire houses,
> and in all of them ... they have their images standing, which be evill
> favoured, made of stone and wood, and some like lions, leopards,
> and monkies; some like men and women, and pecocks; and some
> like the devil with foure arms and 4 hands. (Eck, 1983, pp.9–11)

Whilst it is true that parts of Christian scripture condemn idolatry
(as do the scriptures of some other religions, especially Judaism and
Islam), not all such observers (including Fitch) had sufficient self-
awareness to see that certain Christian acts could be interpreted by
outsiders as idol worship. For example, praying in front of a cross or
the statue of a saint, and facing westwards for the Eucharist, can
seem just as idolatrous as any action of a Hindu or African
traditionalist before her image.

Most religions make a distinction, in their own particular way,
between worship, due only to Transcendent reality, and veneration,
high esteem for a human or other form of revelation on earth. Even
so there is, among the religions, a spectrum of attitude and practice
towards images. At one end are those who believe that no image can
do justice to Transcendence, which is beyond all human forms. In
this category belong Jews, Muslims, early Buddhists, Sikhs and some
Hindus and Christians. Then there are those who regard images as
only symbols; the deity does not dwell within them, but they
remind worshippers of their sacred story; so a Christian may have a
cross in his home and a Buddhist may have an image of the Buddha
or of a boddhisatva. Then there are others who allow images and
claim that a holy person is in some way present: so some Christians
burn a candle to the Virgin Mary or some other saint; and many
Hindus venerate a deity who may be, for them, a manifestation of
the eternal Brahman. Finally, there are lots of people, including
many Hindus, who identify the image with the deity or with some
other manifestation of ultimacy.

No doubt many people who venerate an image are following
their religious instincts rather than acting upon an intellectually
thought-through position. So it is easy to describe such activities as

folk religion. This position often assumes that folk religion is somehow inferior to more deeply considered faithful actions, which may not always be the case.

It is not surprising that some religions are divided about the use of images, since within each religion there are emphases that can point in different directions. For example, Christians believe that God is the high and holy one who inhabits eternity. This suggests that it is impossible to portray him at all. Yet Christians also worship God the Son, the Lord incarnate in Jesus of Nazareth. This indicates that God can be portrayed in human constructs. In the Orthodox Churches of the East, Jesus forms a bridge between God and humanity, heaven and earth, and makes humans become by grace what God is by nature. Jesus is, as it were, the ultimate icon or image of God. Indeed, Christian (and sometimes other) artists, sculptors and musicians have enriched the world with their portrayals of the Christian story. To the secular mind these may simply be great works of art. To the religious imagination, they feed the soul. The great medieval churches, Michelangelo's statue of David or his painting of the Sistine Chapel in the Vatican, Handel's Messiah: these can evoke wonder and even adoration, not just of the human skill behind them but of God whom they depict. Another example from Christianity: most Christians have an act of worship, the Eucharist or Mass or Lord's Supper or Holy Communion, in which bread and wine are used of Jesus the Saviour's body and blood. The word 'of' in the previous sentence masks a great mystery. Are these merely symbols of Jesus' death and resurrection, or something more? Most Christians have argued that they are more than symbols: they are sacraments, signs of the present and coming kingdom of God, showing how God and humans are bound up as participants in the drama of cosmic salvation. How the bread and wine are sacramental has caused much dissension. That they are such is widely held among Christians. So it can be argued that these elements of bread and wine, creations of the human hand, function rather like religious images in locating Transcendence in an extraordinarily powerful way for those who have the eye of faith to see.

Many Hindus believe that Transcendence without a form to evoke it is too remote and that humans therefore need some representation by which to evoke wonder and devotion. So it is not uncommon to hear a Hindu who visits an image simply say, 'I have come to see God'. He sees the image and intuits the boundless ocean of Brahman beyond; and he envisages, with the eye of faith, the deity seeing him and holding him in his creative and sustaining vision.

Even some religions that in theory have very austere views about depicting Transcendence find space in practice for visualising or imaging God's ways in the world. For example, the straight path of Sunni Islam forbids the pictorial representation of God. It frowns upon music and dance. Yet at its edge, certain human constructs celebrate the ways of God among humans. The whirling dervishes of the *mawlawiyya* order, inspired by the great Persian Sufi poet, Jalal al-Din Rumi (1207–73), on one interpretation, attempt in their dancing to imitate the motion of the spheres. The *qawwali* is, even today, a widespread form of music among mystical Sufi Muslims in the South Asian subcontinent, characterised by driving rhythms, explosive clapping, and singing that is full of longing for the divine. Many people claim that *qawwali* heals them of sickness and puts them on the straight path to God.

Music and dance as expressions of the presence and power of God may be marginal activities for many Muslims, or even frowned upon. Yet the art of calligraphy is universal among Muslims. Mosques have artefacts with ornate flourishes in Arabic that link the name of God, Allah, with the seal of the Prophets, Muhammad. In the absence of statues or paintings, calligraphy provides a means of celebrating the divine revelation in human construct. Moreover, many mosques and other buildings are beauteous to behold. The Taj Mahal, built in the seventeenth century near Agra in North India, commemorates the love of the Muslim Emperor Shah Jehan for his dead wife, Mumtaz Mahal, and is truly a wonder of the world.

Among the world's first people, art and aesthetics are important. One example is the 'Vision Quest' of the North American plains aboriginals. This is an ancient, three-fold, rite of passage: that of 'dying', 'passing through' and 'being reborn'. It is a sacred ceremony that culminates in a fast of three days and three nights, alone, in a wilderness place of natural power. Vision may be seen as divers things or interpreted in a number of ways: insight into how things really are; or the ability to dream; or the ability to see the future; or a number of other things. The last long night of the quest leads to a renewal of the solitary self within the wider community, helping the questing person to re-vision who she is in relation to the earth, the spirits, animal life and other humans. This spiritual tradition has now been 'borrowed' by many outsiders. Indeed, it is commonly promoted in New Age circles. If this sometimes makes people think of the Vision Quest as a fad, they should not. At various stages of an American aboriginal's life, it helps her to locate her place in the universe of meaning. For the adolescent, it marks a breakthrough to adult life; for the older person, a transition to a new phase of life, or even a way of contemplating the journey into death. Since it is done in a holy and awesome place, it is a reminder to members of more wordy cultures that spiritual discernment is not confined to what is written or even spoken, but is enabled by what is seen by the eyes and by an inner, more intuitive sense.

holy places

The widespread conviction of the religious imagination that Transcendence can be encountered in art and aesthetics, that is in human artefacts, finds its most particular expression in the belief that certain places especially witness to the presence of Transcendent reality. This section will briefly examine the importance of religious buildings and of pilgrimage in the world's religions.

It is important to define holiness. In many people's minds it has an ethical connotation of extreme goodness or even sanctity. Whilst this is frequently the case, often a specifically ethical dimension may not be at the centre of the meaning of holiness. Primarily, it denotes the presence of the Transcendent in human life. So some places may actually be ethically extremely problematic, yet of extraordinary importance in the aspirations and even the psyche of the worshipper. For example, Jerusalem, which means the 'city of peace', has hardly lived up to its signification, partly and ironically because it has focused the divergent hopes of three world religions, Judaism, Christianity and Islam. As such, it has been invaded and conquered by: Jews under King David who seized it from the Jebusites around 1000 BCE; early Muslims who conquered it in 637 CE and came to see it as the place which the Prophet Muhammad had visited in a vision (Quran 17:1); medieval Christian crusaders who wrested it bloodily from Muslim rule and controlled it from 1099 to 1187 CE, after

which it returned to Muslim rule until the controversial creation of
the modern State of Israel in 1948.

Even so, holy places may indeed evoke in worshippers a sense of the
presence of Transcendence, who is good and caring. Some religions,
often those of first peoples, have no places that are built by human
hands. Rather, their sacred places are often natural objects or
locations: streams, trees and such like. Sometimes, they are artefacts
associated with these places. For example, Dalits, the 'oppressed
ones' of India, outside the caste system, often locate their spirituality
outside Hinduism or any other world religions present in South
Asia. Instead, some worship the image of a mother goddess, often
represented with laden, milk-giving breasts, who is often located
and worshipped near a running stream or some other open space.

However, most religions have a special place or building where
ultimate reality is particularly focused. Jews have synagogues,
Muslims have mosques, Hindus have mandirs or temples, Sikhs
have gurudwaras, and so on. Often, such a place is not just a
worship area but also an important locus of communal gathering.
Indeed, the words 'synagogue' and 'mosque' are among a group of
religious words for a religious building that, in the original
language, indicate a place of gathering.

Psalm 63 verses 1 to 4 gives a taste of the importance of a holy
building for a worshipper. Although this passage has traditionally
been interpreted as a psalm of David, wandering in the wilderness
of Judah during the rebellion of his son Absalom, this is unlikely to
be true. The reference to the sanctuary suggests that the worshipper
has had a deep experience of God in the Temple in Jerusalem:

> O God, you are my God, I seek you, my soul faints for you, as in a dry
> and weary land where there is no water. So I have looked upon you in
> the sanctuary, beholding your power and glory. Because your
> steadfast love is better than life, my lips will praise you. So I will bless
> you as long as I live; I will lift up my hands and call on your name.

Yet specific holy places rarely if ever exhaust the worshipper's
capacity for or ability to worship. He is also expected to worship
elsewhere. For example, many Hindus do not go to the mandir at
all. Even if they do, many have a room or part of a room set aside at
home for *puja*, honour or reverence paid to a deity, the deities or

some aspect of them. Muslims are expected to go to the mosque for Friday midday prayers, but the rest may be said almost anywhere else, except for a few forbidden places. Places of worship are common and commonly used, but they are not always or even often indispensable to their religion. Jews were devastated by the destruction of the First Temple by the Babylonians in 586 BCE, and of the Second by the Romans in 70 CE. The fact that Judaism survived both experiences is because a sufficient number of Jews resisted the notion that God was *only* and *essentially* found in that holy place. So it is that most religions do not insist that a holy place is irreplaceable. Even Christianity, which in some of its forms insists on regular church attendance as a mark of membership, in its early years flourished when Christians were expelled from synagogues and when they had no great churches.

Pilgrimage to holy sites or places is common in religions. Among some religious people, such pilgrimages become metaphors or aspirations rather than actualities. During their long years of exile from their land, Jews would pray at the time of the Passover, 'Next year in Jerusalem'. Few Jews would have been confident of that assertion, though many would have hoped for its fulfilment. Many more would have said it in the spirit of affirming their sense of peoplehood and their trust that God would one day be faithful to the promises he had made to their ancestors. Another example is the spirituals of enslaved black African Christians in the USA before the Civil War, many of which evoked the language of Canaan, Zion and the Jordan River as symbols of heavenly glory after earthly tribulation.

Sometimes the metaphor of pilgrimage is rooted in the earliest origins of a religion. An example is the importance of Luke's writings at the beginning of Christian history. His Gospel begins in Palestine, far from Rome, the political centre of things. Yet it hints at the concerns of the wider world: for example, Jesus is born on a journey undertaken by Mary and Joseph during a general registration of the Roman world (Luke 2:1ff.). By the end of Luke's second work, Acts of Apostles, the good news has moved from humble and obscure origins to the religious centre of Jerusalem, and thereafter, within about thirty years to the Imperial, secular capital of Rome. So the Gospel and Acts are about journeys. Of course, there is a historical dimension to this emphasis. The news of Jesus did spread with amazing rapidity in the first century, helped by the unified Roman Empire, which by and large maintained peace within its borders, and built good roads on which to travel. Sea journeys were more perilous, but still possible. Yet Luke's emphasis upon the theme of journeying was not simply an attempt to be historically accurate. He had other points than historical ones to make. He wanted to emphasise that individual believers must be personally involved in the tales they tell, since each is a pilgrim in the way of Jesus. Each must take up her cross daily and follow him (Luke 9:23). The word 'daily' is Luke's addition to the saying. It does not water down a difficult, specific reference to Jesus' cruel death on the cross, by generalising it. Rather, it is an integral part of Luke's conviction that the Christlike life (the believer's imitation of Christ is important to him) is a daily journey of the heart, soul, strength and mind. Luke's metaphor of pilgrimage has resounded through Christian history. Until recently, after the Bible one of the most popular works in Britain was John Bunyan's *Pilgrim's Progress*, first published in 1678, the fictitious story of Pilgrim's travel through 'the wilderness of this world' to 'the other side'. Its debt to Luke's theme of religious journeying is considerable. (See further: Forward, 1998b, pp.26–32)

Lots of religious people make actual journeys, or intend to. Many Hindus hope to die in Varanasi, also known as Banaras, Hindu India's holiest city. There, they can be cremated and their ashes wash away on Mother Ganga, the holy River Ganges. A significant number achieve this goal. Muslims hope to make the trip to Mecca once in their lifetime, during the month of pilgrimage. Lots of them fulfil this dream. In each case, pilgrims believe that the presence and power of ultimate reality is specifically located in a certain place or area. Roman Catholics (and others) go to Lourdes and hope for healing; Theravada Buddhists (and others) visit the temple at Kandy in Sri Lanka, which preserves a tooth of the Buddha, and are powerfully reminded of the Buddha's message of liberation; and so on.

Religious people are sometimes misguided or superstitious in their enterprise of journeying. Often it is other religious people who are quick to see this and point it out. The Buddha scorned much pilgrimage as meaningless ritual, declaring that: 'If the waters of the Ganges could truly wash away sin then all fishes would go straight to heaven.' The Englishman Geoffrey Chaucer (*c.*1340–1400), in his

Sunrise at the River Ganges in Varanasi (Banaras), India. Sadhus *(holy men) perform ablutions praising the rising sun and the river goddess, Ganga. (Photograph, Nancy M. Martin. Reproduced, with permission, from* The Meaning of Life in the World Religions. *Oxford, Oneworld, 2000)*

The Canterbury Tales, cast a jaundiced eye upon the motives, unworthy thoughts and impious actions of many pilgrims to the shrine of Thomas à Becket. His was a hilarious and profound act of mockery. Many would retort that, even if it were true that some pilgrims are gullible and others ill intentioned, that does not condemn the enterprise. At its best, a religious pilgrimage is a profoundly moving and transformative experience for participants. For example, Muslims who return from pilgrimage in Mecca, Medina and the environs during the appropriate month, often radiate joy and serenity as they relate their experiences. Similarly, many of the Christian pilgrims whom Chaucer amusingly ridiculed would have gone, not as lechers on the lookout for casual sex, or pickpockets or avaricious merchants hoping to cash in on human gullibility, but 'with a broken and a contrite heart' (Psalm 51:17).

In many cases, the experience of the pilgrim is focused on certain prescribed routes he must take, artefacts he must see, or things he must do with others. For example, Muslim pilgrims to Mecca are obliged to wear certain clothing and undertake certain routes and acts. (These are helpfully summarised in Robinson, 1999, pp.127–148.) Holiness is not usually noticed by tourists, especially those who rush from place to place, thus displaying the mentality of 'If it's Tuesday, we must be in Belgium'.

Religious tourism is perhaps problematic. For example, many contemporary secularised Christians who 'do' the Holy Land see nothing of religious importance at all, as religions interpret 'importance'. But some are overwhelmed by the experience. Such tourism is not new, and neither is criticism of it. The Roman Horace, a century before Jesus, wrote: '*Caelum non animum mutant qui trans mare currunt*', 'They change their clime, not their frame of mind, who cross the sea'. Ancient India had a highly developed religious tourist industry, with both excited partakers and cynical critics. Sometimes keen-eyed participants showed both characteristics. The Chinese Buddhist pilgrim Fa-hsien left his home in Chang-an in 399 CE in search of *dharma* ('duty' or 'righteousness'). He crossed Central Asia and North India, then went by sea to Sri Lanka and Java. He returned to China in 412. He noted a widespread cult of relics all across the Buddhist world. Similar examples could be given of Christian pilgrims about the same time, and, at a later date, of Muslim and other religious voyagers.

holy word

Many people think that scripture is the most important channel of communication between ultimate reality and humankind. That may be true for Muslims and Sikhs, arguably for Orthodox Jews and for certain Protestant Christians. But it is by no means universally held to be so by members of the world's religions. We have noted that most religions of the first people of the world, in Africa, North America and elsewhere, do not have any scriptures, yet their adherents certainly believe that the great beyond draws near to them. Moreover, even in scripturally dominated religions like Islam, the holy writ needs an interpreter or interpretations. Furthermore, mainstream Christian faith has regarded scripture as the secondary revelation, pointing to the primary revelation of Jesus the Christ.

So it is worth reflecting that scripture is not the only way by which people receive revelation from the unseen world, and are constituted and strengthened in their life of faith. Surely there is a point here for scriptural literalists. Scripture is one of a number of signs pointing to Transcendent reality and its demands on human beings. It is a means, not an end in itself, in the central teachings of the world's religions.

It is also worth reflecting that for most people in the past and for lots in the present, scripture is uttered rather than read. For example, when a Christian says 'This is the word of the Lord' after a biblical reading in church, she is affirming something important about orality and aurality: scripture read *to* us, not by us, and heard, not looked at. To give a personal example: I know from my own experience how remarkable and transformative the hearing of scripture can be. As a young boy, I heard a record of the Welsh actor Richard Burton reading the story of King David waiting for and receiving the news of his son Absalom's death (2 Sam. 18:24–33). I was on the edge of my chair with excitement: in my imagination, I too scanned the horizon, along with the watchman, to hear the messenger of tidings, good or ill. I wept with the old king and father, as he stumbled away from the story, wounded to the heart at the moment of his triumph. I have read it many times since. I only come close to that first hearing when, as worship leader, I read it in church, and witness its power to move on the faces of people before me, three thousand years later yet right there in God's eternal now. Such is the glory of scripture: to link time with eternity, to catch us up in an ultimate vision that can then sustain, enrich and illuminate our mundane existence.

This illustration raises the importance of scripture as an oral or recited text. Many literate Westerners think of scripture as something to be read, but for most people, whether in worship or some other context, it is spoken and heard. In Arabic, Quran means 'recitation'. The Prophet Muhammad, believed by most Muslims to have been illiterate, received God's word in a powerful intuitive way, for which 'hearing' would be a much closer approximation than 'reading'. This is true, despite the fact that Islam is associated in many people's mind with an emphasis upon the written book. Only some time after Muhammad's death was the Quran compiled in written form as we have it today. Even today, Muslims who memorise the Quran and can chant it by heart (known as *hafiz*) are regarded with awe and respect by other Muslims. On the 'Night of Power', in the month of fasting, a date that celebrates the first reception of revelation by Muhammad, many Muslims spend the night in a mosque to *hear* a *hafiz* recite God's word. Similar illustrations could be given of the importance of the oral experience of the word in Judaism, Hinduism, Sikhism and Buddhism. Indeed, one can argue for the primacy of the oral reception of scripture in the religious experience of humankind (Coward, 2000, *passim*).

Still, in many but not all religions, written scripture is of great importance. (Indeed, the word scripture comes from one meaning 'writing'.) One major factor that leads to the creation of a written scripture is the fear that the oral may be lost or even 'contaminated' by interpolated and false information. So one must not downplay the importance of holy books for many of the world's religious people. There are two particular factors that comprise the 'holiness' of a sacred book. First, there is its witness to, in some cases as a direct message from, Transcendent reality. Secondly, there is its reception by individual believers and religious communities to constitute and maintain their life of faith.

To illustrate from Christian faith, about the two particular factors of divine revelation and human appropriation: the Bible is holy because Christians believe it is a gift from God for his people; but unless Christian people lay hold of it in their heart, their soul and their mind, it is powerless to save, or, indeed, to effect any other genuine religious function.

There are some Christians who think that we should excise bits from scripture that offend modern sensibilities, and add tone to what is left by laying alongside it some other literary classics. In his last years, the distinguished Methodist preacher, Leslie Weatherhead, came to believe strongly that parts of scripture are not profitable for modern people. So, for example, he wrote that 'it must be admitted that much of the Old Testament is dull, meaningless, irrelevant and hopelessly sub-Christian in its sentiments' (1965, p.147). Not many Jews would agree with the first half of this sentence, and would deem the bit about being sub-Christian an irrelevant impertinence. Thirty years on, Weatherhead's interpretation seems to reflect the sad excesses of a man who has seen the hollowness of much liberal theology, but not quite seen through it. So he attempts to rescue it by a somewhat intemperate attack on holy writ. Best let holy writ stand, warts and all, to question us more than we, it. The Bible plays a uniquely constitutive and sustaining role in transforming Christians. Much as many literate English Christians love Shakespeare and learn a great deal from him about divine grace and the human condition, for them Shakespeare does not play the same role as the Bible does.

Indeed, there are all sorts of reasons why excising passages of scripture or adding other literary classics to it, is a profitless exercise. The major reason is that scripture is, in the belief of most religious people, a numinous document whose purpose is to challenge humans, rather than they challenge it. So, for example, Christians believe the Bible to be a gift from God for his people, appropriated by the Church to constitute and maintain its life and faith.

In what way or ways is scripture a gift from God for his people? One common belief has been to maintain that it is precisely God's word, transmitted to human beings.

At one point in the development of Hindu faith, scriptures were divided into *shruti* and *smriti*. *Shruti*, 'heard' works, are distinguished from *smriti*, 'remembered' works. *Shruti* works, the most sacred and, if you like 'inspired' scriptures, the Vedas and Upanishads, were 'heard' from the gods by ancient seers and sages. Even so, the Bhagavad Gita, spoken of as *smriti*, or remembered, has long been regarded on the same high plane as *shruti* works. Therefore, there may be a warning here that one should not read too much out of, or into, this twofold distinction.

In China, the Tao Tsang comprises about 1120 volumes, about two hundred of which were in existence by the seventh century CE; in all, they were compiled over about fifteen centuries. Some of these books claim to be divine revelations made to Taoist adepts whilst in a trance-like state. Perhaps it is worth pointing out that some individuals even today, not just in China but elsewhere, claim to be in receipt of what seems, in some sense, like divine revelation. For example, the illiterate Indian Sikh leader, Baba Virsa Singh, has had a vision of and conversation with Jesus. At his farm just outside Delhi, he and his devotees have built a place in honour of Jesus at the spot where this vision occurred.

The Orthodox Jewish view is that God conveyed the Pentateuch, the five books of Moses, directly and in its entirety to Moses, with the possible exception of the account of Moses' death at the end of Deuteronomy. The rabbis referred to it as 'Torah from Heaven', the very word of God – teachings, laws, doctrines and rules of life from the creator of the universe. This 'Torah from Heaven' has been passed on in a continuing chain of tradition ever since. The later expositions and elaborations of scripture by the rabbis in the Mishnah, the Talmud, and indeed all the later teachings, were also believed to be delivered by God to Moses on Sinai: this is Oral Torah. As it happens, many contemporary non-Orthodox Jews see this as a kind of 'myth of origins'. They embrace the historical-critical method as forcefully as have many Christians. Indeed, many Orthodox Jews are willing to concede a human involvement in other parts of their scripture, but recoil from attributing it to the Pentateuch itself.

In Islam, there has similarly been an unwillingness, indeed often a flat refusal, to attribute a human element to divine revelation. Muslims believe that from about the year 610 until his death in 632, the Prophet Muhammad received piecemeal, at irregular intervals, and through the medium of the angel Jibril or Gabriel, God's own word. When Muhammad died, Abu Bakr succeeded him as the political head of the Muslim community, but his spiritual authority as transmitter of God's word died with him. The traditional view, now challenged but not yet quite overturned, is that the Quran was collected together in the form we now have it, which is not chronological, when Uthman was the third caliph, or political successor to Muhammad, between 644 and 656.

Many contemporary Muslims still believe that the Quran is precisely God's word, on the grounds that it guarantees the divine origin of Islam. The contemporary erstwhile anthropologist and Pakistani diplomat, thereafter Cambridge don, Akbar Ahmed recounts a story of being interviewed with another academic on a TV programme:

> 'You keep on saying to Akbar ... why don't you accept the human origin of your religion? Well, he can't,' Ernest Gellner [formerly Professor of Social Anthropology at the University of Cambridge] said sharply, coming to my rescue, in a television discussion on Islam. 'Islam has not,' he further explained, 'been secularized. This is the great mystery about it. All the other world religions have been softened, have permitted ambiguities of meanings.' Gellner was right [writes Akbar Ahmed]. For those who believe in Islam, the choice is between being Muslim and being nothing: there is no other choice. (Ahmed, 1992, p.42)

Gellner supports a common Muslim view, reaffirmed by Akbar Ahmed, but whether it is credible, or simply a matter of unexamined but widespread belief and assertion, is debatable. After all, subtlety, ambiguities of meanings, and pluralism of commitments are not unknown within Islam.

What is clear, however, is how few Muslims have felt able to question the Quran's status as the exact and unambiguous Word of God. In differentiating Semitic from Greek views about God, Ahmed writes that 'God on high spoke through chosen prophets and the divine words were embodied in holy books: the Jewish and Christian scriptures and the Quran' (1992, p.57). Some Jews and Christians have reinterpreted how God is revelatory in their scriptures, not so as to exclude divine participation in the process, but so that human contributions can also be upheld. This has not been a route trodden by many Muslims. A very few Muslim Modernists from the South Asian sub-continent have raised this matter. Most of them have done so tentatively.

One startling exception was the Indian judge, and, in 1910, the first Indian member of the Privy Council, Syed Ameer Ali. As early as 1873, he published a book which maintained that:

> A careful study of the Koran makes it evident that the mind of Mohammed went through the same process of development which marked the religious consciousness of Jesus... The various chapters of the Koran which contain the ornate descriptions of paradise, whether figurative or literal, were delivered wholly or in part at Mecca. Probably in the infancy of his religious consciousness Mohammed himself believed in some or other of the traditions which floated around him. But with a wider awakening of the soul, a deeper communion with the Spirit of the Universe, thoughts which bore a material aspect at first became spiritualised. (1873, pp.281f.)

Ameer Ali's view of the provenance of the Quran, associating it with the mind of Muhammad, a view that he never changed, is quite unacceptable to orthodox Muslim belief. What is particularly telling is that this interesting association is not justified or developed in any way. He seems to assume that everyone will know about and accept this interpretation. He hardly reveals a clear and open desire to reinterpret his own tradition creatively and provocatively.

What exactly was Ameer Ali doing, then? It is extraordinary that he did not admit the singularity and unorthodox nature of his conviction, if only as a prelude to making his case for arguing that it (or some of it) expresses the mind of Muhammad. Thus, though it is possible that he was trying, clumsily and simplistically, and with too much reliance upon nineteenth-century European notions of the progressive development of humankind, to restate orthodox views in ways that his audience could appreciate and affirm, it is also arguable that he was, in crucially important respects, ignorant of what constitutes orthodox Islamic belief. At any rate, the fact that few Muslims picked him up on this point over the half-century in which he continued to make it, shows how few have read him carefully. (Forward, 1999, p.40)

Even if most Muslims, unlike Ameer Ali, hold fast to the divine *origin* and *transmission* of the Quran, some have provided innovative ways of understanding the human *reception* and *meaning* of it. These may open up new possibilities of engagement with scholars who advocate a more critical engagement with the understanding of sacred texts.

Fazlur Rahman, a Pakistani Muslim who died in 1988, raises this issue. His statement that 'the Prophet could have... indulged in merely grandiose formulas' hints at the unorthodox view that the Prophet rather than God is the author of the Quran. His view is in fact an attempt to hold together both God's and the Prophet's involvement in the revelation. In his chapter on the Quran, he argues that: '[Muslim] orthodoxy (indeed, all medieval thought) lacked the necessary intellectual tools to combine in its formulation of the dogma [of the nature of Revelation] the otherness and verbal character of the Revelation on the one hand, and its intimate connection with the work and the religious personality of the Prophet on the other, i.e. it lacked the intellectual capacity to say both that the Quran is entirely the Word of God and, in an ordinary sense, also entirely the word of Muhammad. The Quran obviously holds both, for if it insists that it has come to the "heart" of the Prophet, how can it be external to him?' Fazlur Rahman goes on to argue that Muslim orthodoxy 'made the Revelation of the Prophet entirely through the ear and external to him and regarded the angel or the spirit "that comes to the heart" an entirely external agent. The modern Western picture of the Prophetic Revelation rests largely on this orthodox formulation rather than on the Quran, as does, of course, the belief of the common Muslim.' (Rahman, 1979, p.31f.)

The divine, or, if you like, Transcendent, origin of scripture is universally believed. However, to maintain that scripture is dictated by a Transcendent reality is not the only way of interpreting its importance and authority. Even when this belief is firmly held by someone, he has then to reflect on its meaning in the life of that person or those people to whom it was given and, just as important, in his own life and for the wider world in which he presently lives.

This is where the second part of my definition of the importance of scripture comes into play. Scripture must be appropriated by communities of faith, as transformative documents. Scriptures transform communities and individuals of faith, because they communicate with, interpret, intuit supramundane, transcendent reality. Theists would call that Transcendent reality, God. Others would not.

The most notable example of a religion in which God or the gods are, at bottom, irrelevant is Buddhism. Many Buddhists believe in the gods, but they are, to use a Christian phrase, powerless to save. To put it in a Buddhist way, the gods are caught up in the round of this earth's ages, in the process of becoming and re-becoming through many births. They, too, need to be liberated to the truth about things. Gautama Siddharth became the Buddha, the awakened or enlightened one, for this age. About six centuries before Jesus, he tried a number of ways of enlightenment; including asceticism and prayer; but saw through them all. Then, seated beneath a Bo tree, he saw the light. He woke up. The penny dropped. He was able to interpret the world, the universe, as they really are. Out of compassion for humanity, he did not immediately enter the bliss of *nirvana*, but taught human beings the way through suffering, due to our inappropriate attachments.

Some non-Buddhists describe Buddhism as a philosophy rather than a religion. That is to miss the point that Buddhists aspire to see beyond this world's apparent meanings, to the truth of how things really and eternally are. Now, theists may wish to have frank and comradely discussion with Buddhists about different perceptions of that truth; whether it is the same truth; or whether both have it wrong; or whatever. My present point is that Buddhists believe that there *is* a Transcendent reality, more real and enduring than the sensory world we inhabit. In their view, the devices and desires of our own hearts often lure us into granting this world more reality than it really possesses. We need to wake up to our real possibilities.

So scriptures exist for Buddhists as a means of evoking either the Buddha's achievement, or the attainments of other enlightened beings, or in describing that world of Transcendent reality. In many cases, different Buddhist groupings can be defined by the scripture they possess, and which possesses them. So, for example, the Lotus Sutra, more properly the *Saddharma Pundarika*, or 'True Law Lotus', is the favourite Mahayana Buddhist scripture. It was written in Sanskrit early in the Christian era, widely translated and used in China, Japan and elsewhere. It has been called 'the Gospel of half-Asia'. It depicts the exalted Buddha on a Himalayan peak, giving a new vehicle of universal liberation; this offends some monks who withdraw; the Buddha then proceeds to develop his teachings of what, to a Christian, looks extraordinarily like the Protestant reformer Martin Luther's doctrine of salvation by faith. The twenty-fourth chapter, often recited by Zen and other Buddhists, tells of the grace of the compassionate Boddhisatva Avalokiteshvara, who is praised by the Buddha for bestowing many benefits upon his worshippers. This Boddhisatva, which means 'a being destined for enlightenment', is found in many forms in East Asia. Tibetan Buddhists regard the Dalai Lama as a reincarnation of him.

holy people

There are some people who seem to know and reveal the Transcendent in their lives (however that reality is defined in particular religions). Just as holy places are holy because of their connection with Transcendent power and presence rather than with an indispensably ethical content, so it often is the case with holy people. When we examine the life of the Muslim Rabia al-Adawiyya or the Christian Francis of Assisi or the Hindu Mahatma Gandhi, we might be greatly impressed by their moral integrity. If we reflect a little further, we would recognise that this arose out of the strong sense they and others had that ultimate Transcendent reality undergirded and transformed their lives. Devotees may venerate holy people in the form of pictures or statues or even, in their lifetime, by following them faithfully or seeking them out in the belief that their presence is inspirational and even healing. Many such saints, however, are very aware of their own shortcomings; sometimes they appear to be right to do so; it is the search for the divine and their own response to it that is at the heart of their aspirations and of their appeal to others. To search for the clay feet of saints is to miss the point, even though, in this world of sin and ignorance, you will surely find them.

Some religions have groups of people who particularly focus the presence of Transcendence. Often such people have no great personal charisma (although some may do) but are professional holy people. These are sometimes functionaries of a religious building. So rabbis are attached to synagogues, priests to churches, imams to mosques, and so on. Again, the holiness associated with them is not chiefly to do with the moral worth of their lives though some may be good. Rather, they perform certain actions that remind people powerfully of ultimate reality. These actions vary within each tradition. Christian clergy usually preside at worship, and often have an important role to play in religious teaching, in visiting worshippers and other people, and in the running of the building. Traditionally, rabbis also have a major responsibility in worship and educational matters, but much less responsibility for pastoral care and for the non-worship work of the synagogue. Imams are closer to rabbis than to Christian priests in this matter. In Hindu Temples and Sikh gurudwaras, the cultic figure has even less say in other than worship and educational matters. Most such figures are men. The first Christian clergywoman was ordained in the USA in 1853. Women rabbis are much more recent. In both cases, strong groups within each religion regard the ordination of women (or its equivalent) as inappropriately innovative. Although in Islam women can lead other women in communal prayer, they do not characteristically act as prayer leader (*imam*) for men or for mixed groups of worshippers.

Religions also have holy people who are not associated as worship leaders with a certain place or places. Christianity and Buddhism have monks and nuns, though Islam condemns this practice. The Buddha ordained women, but hesitated at first. His aunt, Queen Mahapajapati, with five hundred women from the court, asked him for ordination. Some Buddhists have regarded his initial scepticism as a sign of reluctance. Others have seen it as a recognition of prevalent social factors that would inhibit the full acceptance of women. This last group believes he finally agreed to ordain women on the grounds that they had as much potential for enlightenment as men.

In many indigenous communities, there is an intermediary to the spirit world. He or she regulates relationships within the community and between it and the spirit world. In Siberia, this figure was called the shaman, and this term is now widely used for centrally important holy people among the first people. The shaman's responsibilities may include, for example, ensuring that a harmonious balance is maintained between the worlds of humans, the rest of creation, and the spirits.

When do people take up holiness? Pragmatically, Hinduism has encouraged people to consider eternal matters towards the end of their lives. Traditionally, it locates four stages of life. The first is that of a student. This period ends with marriage and the new stage of householder. When his children grow up, a person should become a 'forest-dweller', as should his wife, and pursue non-worldly activities. Finally, he should renounce home and possessions, wandering as a beggar from one holy place to another as a *samnyasa*. Although this is rarely followed by married people today, there are a large number of *sadhus* ('good, holy persons'), in many different orders. Most no longer wander around but are attached to a monastery where they live simple and dedicated lives. Some Hindus are devoted to a *guru* ('teacher'), a spiritual instructor who has attained spiritual insights that he or she can pass on to the pupil. He or she can enlighten others and help them to cross the ocean of repeated death and birth (*samsara*) and so achieve liberation (*moksha*).

Just as criticisms have been made of the greed and gullibility of people in relation to holy places, so certain (often self-appointed) holy people are repellent to thoughtful observers. Some media-obsessed Christian broadcasters in the USA and elsewhere seem to be little more than con artists. Similarly, in the last thirty or so years many relatively prosperous young (and not so young) Europeans have visited India for enlightenment, and have been credulous victims of greedy gurus; this has been brilliantly outlined by Gita Mehta in her hilarious book *Karma Cola* (1981). Of course, not all such religious practitioners are rogues, but a surprisingly large number seem to be. It is a useful rule, when dealing with such claimants to supranatural authority, to ask if they want money or sex. If they do, they are not true gurus. The more such individuals benefit personally from their activities, the more sceptical one should be: Moses, the Buddha, Zoroaster, Jesus, Muhammad, Guru Nanak, Baha'ul'lah and other such holy figures do not seem to have gained much personal financial profit from their teachings. Some other credible figures have made money, but have not used it to fund a lavish life-style.

These foundational religious figures are the most important of all holy people. Many religions (with the important exception of certain of the religions of first people) focus on the veneration of one or a number of people, whose lives are often embellished.

Hinduism has a variety of such figures, one of the most important of whom is Lord Krishna. *Bhakti* mystics ardently love and worship God as personal. The worship of Krishna is an especially important example of *bhakti* devotion. *Bhakti* comes from a Sanskrit word meaning 'to share', so *bhakti* is relational love shared by the deity and the devotee. Many Hindus take the notion of the 'down-coming' of the god into the image very seriously indeed. The image is a manifestation of the Supreme Lord, who entrusts himself to the care of humans. So Hindus wash images and look after them with great reverence as a sign that the image is a divine guest to whom hospitality is due.

Although some people believe Krishna to be a wholly legendary figure, his birthplace is located in a number of sites and many Hindus fervently believe the tales about him. The Buddha, Jesus and Muhammad are more clearly figures who actually lived and died, yet modern historical criticism suggests that their lives have also been significantly interpreted and even embellished by their followers.

These figures are venerated differently in each religion; sometimes, within different interpretations of the same faith. Most Buddhists do not treat the Buddha as a god; they meditate upon him in order to focus upon his enlightenment that provides inspiration, helping them to wake up to the true reality of things. The vast majority of Jews do not venerate Moses; still less do they worship him. Rather, they acknowledge him as the prophet of the exodus from Egypt, to whom God gave scripture on Sinai. Sikhs now treat their scripture as the living guru, to which they prostrate at worship in the gurudwara. This continues the reverence, even worship, they offered to the ten gurus of mainstream Sikhism, who ceased with Guru Gobind Sigh (d.1708); he declared that the Adi Granth, scripture itself, would be the continuing guru (which means 'teacher'). Christians worship Jesus as the only Son of God, Lord and Saviour.

So foundational figures are honoured differently in each religion. Christianity is closer to religions of South Asia (Buddhism, Hinduism, Jainism and others) in its belief that the divine takes human form, than it is to Judaism and Islam, the other monotheistic Semitic faiths. Yet Christians admit only one incarnation of God in human flesh, whereas many Hindus believe in many 'down comings' of the gods when human wickedness demands it.

Sometimes these figures are claimed by more than one religion. This may appear to offer potentially creative links between faiths, but this is rarely the case. The variant interpretations often divide religions. So, for example, some Hindus regard the Buddha as an incarnation of Lord Vishnu; ironically, given the Buddha's scepticism about the power of gods to help their devotees achieve enlightenment. Muslims regard Jesus as Messiah, but deny that he is Son of God and Saviour, thus denuding him of his central importance for Christians. In each of these cases, a figure is foundational for one religion but not for the other. Some Hindus may revere the Buddha, but he is not a centrally important figure in Hinduism. Jesus may be held in esteem by Muslims, but he is not of crucial significance to their faith in the way that Muhammad or even Abraham is.

the mystical path

The foundational figures of many religions seem to have had a strong knowledge of the existence and character of Transcendence. In the case of a figure like the Buddha, as he sat under the Bo Tree, the scales fell from his eyes and he saw through the impermanence of this world to the enduring reality of how things actually are. Some foundational figures did not see the world in the rather impersonal way of the Buddha and his followers.

The Prophet Muhammad received revelation from and about the one God, who, though majestic and quite other than humans, revealed his will to them. The remarkable throne-verse from the Quran 2:255 illustrates this. In later developments, Muslim mystics saw Muhammad as the first of their fraternity. They point to his night journey (in Arabic, *miraj*) from Mecca to Jerusalem, when he passed through the seven heavens, accompanied by Gabriel. At each stage, they saw a great prophet, last of all, Abraham. Reflecting later upon this, Muhammad is said to have stated: 'I was a prophet when Adam was still between water and clay.' The summit of the ascent was a lote-tree. Muslim mystics hold that Gabriel could not pass with Muhammad beyond the lote-tree, lest he burn his wings. This is a reminder that every veil and hindrance (even an archangel) must be torn away to leave the lover alone with his beloved. (Forward, 1997, pp.43–46)

Many Muslims believe that, although Muhammad was 'the seal of the prophets' (Quran 33:40), Jesus was 'the seal of the saints'. The Christian Gospels describe how Jesus called God 'Father', and encouraged his closest followers to do so in the Lord's Prayer (Matt. 6:9–13; Luke 11:2–4). Jesus addressed God by the Aramaic word *Abba*, which has a tenderness and intimacy that are breathtaking, considering that it is used by a creature of the universal creator. Jesus observed that God counts every hair of a human head, a wonderfully exaggerated image of the close care ultimate reality takes of all that she has made.

Such figures seem to have a remarkably close knowledge of how things really are and even, when the religion holds this to be possible and appropriate, a recognition that ultimate reality is personal and can be related to, closely, affectionately and tenderly. They have had many followers. Indeed, they and their disciples hold out the hope that the difference between their experiences and the more mundane attempts of the majority of humankind to find Transcendence, is one of degree, not of kind.

Mystical experiences do not usually happen casually or in hit-or-miss fashion. To be sure, the Christian apostle Paul had a sudden, unexpected and even unwelcome vision of the exalted Christ on the road to Damascus, where he intended to root out Christian deviants (as he thought of them up until that moment). Thereafter, however, he seems to have had strongly mystical experiences built upon a

profound intention to work at the meaning of that vision for his life
and the lives of many (Acts 9:1–19; 2 Cor. 12:1–10).

Like human relations, that between a human and the great
beyond has to be worked at. In Christianity, over time this way has
been divided into three momentous stages through which the
aspirant must pass in order to achieve union with God. This is akin
to a *scala perfectionis*, a 'ladder of perfection', which begins with the
purgative life, the way of purification. Through detachment,
renunciation and asceticism, the devotee moves from the world of
the self and the senses to the ultimate reality of God. This stripping
away leads to the illuminative life, wherein she lovingly contemplates
God in a state of happy and contented awareness of mystery and
ignorance. Then the highest stage is the unitive life, an intoxicating,
joyful state of utter bliss. Some see this as a marriage between the
soul and God. In the Eastern Churches, this whole pilgrimage of the
soul is interpreted as deification. There are parallels here with the
Muslim concept of *fana* (which we shall shortly discuss; there was
much mutual influence between Muslim and Eastern Christian
mystics), including the tightrope act mystics performed before
(often self-appointed) mainstream believers who felt that the
ultimate mystical experience compromised monotheism. No doubt
some mystics have left behind doctrinal orthodoxy, or at least (in
their opinion) seen through it as a hindrance rather than a help.
However, much of this debate is an argument over language. The
mystics had reached a point where human language simply broke
down as an effective means of describing what was happening in
their lives. The point, as they saw it, was a participative process of
experiencing and enjoying God, not a meticulous role of describing a
process from the outside stance of an onlooker.

In Hinduism devotees of the yoga ('yoke') tradition have sought
the goal of *samandhi*, or becoming one with the Transcendent.
There are various forms of yoga. Patanjali (scholars debate his life
span, with dates from the second century BCE to the fifth century CE
being given) founded *Raja-yoga* (the 'royal' way), also known as
Samkhya-yoga because of its connection with one of the six (and
possibly the oldest) systems of orthodox Hindu philosophy. This
taught a mastery of the mind. Yoga has taught the importance of
breath control, which leads its practitioners to stages of realisation.
The most famous Hindu philosopher of the Vedanta school (the

sixth and most important system of philosophy), Shankara (c.788–820 CE), taught a strict non-dualism. Thus, he interpreted the famous phrase *Tat Tvam Asi*, 'That thou art', to indicate that each person is one with the reality behind all things. Hindus have indeed differed about the nature of ultimate reality as monistic (all are part of the great 'oneness' of being) or dualistic (Transcendence is conceived as being other than humans), or some intermediate position or positions. So mystical Hindus from these different traditions differ about how they share in or relate to the great reality whose truth they seek to realise by their practices.

Other sorts of religious people have sometimes regarded mystics as rather élitist; more self-absorbed than absorbed by or in God. No doubt some have been so. Yet people of a mystical turn of mind have sometimes led great religious revolutions, as foundational religious figures like the Buddha, Jesus and Muhammad so clearly illustrate.

Furthermore, many great mystics have been women. This subverts the religious mainstream, which has characteristically been male-dominated and highly patriarchal. An early Muslim woman mystic, Rabia al-Adawiyya (d. 801 CE) passed all her life in Basra, a major city now in Southern Iraq. She was enslaved as a child, and became an ascetic when released. She emphasised the love of God, refusing marriage and preferring rather to be beloved of God. When asked what was the basis of her faith, she replied:

> I have not served God from fear of hell, for I should be like a wretched hireling, if I did it from fear; nor from love of Paradise, for I should be a bad servant if I loved for the sake of what was given, but I have served Him only for the Love of Him and the Desire of Him. (Smith, 1994, p.125)

Some contemporaries ascribed to her these words:

> I have loved thee with two loves, a selfish love and a love that is worthy. As for the love which is selfish, I occupy myself therein with remembrance of Thee to the exclusion of all others. As to that which is worthy of Thee, therein Thou raisest the veil that I may see Thee. Yet there is no praise to me in this or that. But the praise is to Thee, whether in that or this. (Smith, 1994, p.126)

Subversion of mainstream positions is, to some extent, characteristic of mystical experience. Hinduism furnishes many examples of important women mystics, who rode roughshod over certain male notions of how they should behave. Mirabai was a Rajput princess from Chitor, a poet. She lived from *c.*1547–*c.*1614. Married young, she was widowed in 1565. She was devoted to the Lord Krishna but also to a low caste saint, Raidas, a fifteenth-century leather-worker, forty-one of whose hymns are now found in the Sikh scripture. Her devotional works (which often mock unnecessary asceticism) are full of passionate addresses to Krishna:

> I am thirsting for your love, my Beloved!
> I shall make this body a lamp, and my tender heart shall be its wick;
> I shall fill it with the scented oil of my young love and burn it night and day at Your shrine, O Beloved!
> For your love I shall sacrifice all the wealth of my youth;
> Your name shall be the crown of my head. (Appleton, 1988, p.291)

Mirabai went to live at temples dedicated to Krishna at Vrindaban and the Dwarka where, so legend has it, an image of Krishna came to life and disappeared with her into the earth.

In Islam, Sunni orthodoxy has stressed the importance of obeying the will of God, revealed through the Quran and developing religious law. Muslim mystics have preferred obedience to a different vision. They have located a number of stages on the way of mysticism, by which the mystic reaches his goal of *fana*, 'passing away', 'annihilation'. There has been some heated intra-Islamic debate whether some Muslims believed this was the cessation of self, like Buddhist aspirations in achieving *nirvana*, or the continuation of the self in God. Many Muslims (especially those who considered themselves mainstream) were shocked by the implication that the self and God could, in some sense, be one. They were not always sufficiently aware of the mystics' disapproval of them and their lower-order aspiration simply to locate and obey God's will. Mystics seem, rather, to ask: why be like a servant when you could dance in the glow of God's sun? The great thirteenth-century Muslim mystic, Rumi, who celebrated the universal love of God, used this image. He was also careful to stress his attachment to mainstream Islam, maintaining that he 'has not spoken and will not speak words of infidelity: do not disbelieve him'. (Forward, 1997, p.49) It is a moot point whether he was merely deflecting criticism, or really meant what he said.

Until quite recently, Islamic mysticism has been regarded by many as a marginal and eccentric activity. This is not the case. For example, in South Asia it is far more important to ordinary believers than many of the tenets of Sunni Islam. To be sure, mysticism sometimes descends into superstition and folk-religion. But often, when people resort to *pirs* (holy people), either living or dead, to intercede for children or some other boon, their actions imply a profound sense of *tawhid*, the unity of God, which lies at the heart of the Islamic revelation. All things are bound together in God's oneness, yet certain places and people can particularly focus his presence and his power so may be approached as a means of encountering ultimacy.

In Judaism, mysticism is much less deeply rooted than in some other religions, yet it has an important place. The mystical system of Kabbalah (which, significantly, means 'tradition') developed in the eleventh and twelfth centuries; especially in twelfth-century Provence among the followers of Isaac the Blind. The Zohar was compiled at the end of the thirteenth century as the major exposition of secret lore. For some Jews, it is sacred, alongside the Hebrew Bible and the Talmud. Kabbalists argued that there are two aspects of deity: God as he is in himself and God as he reveals himself. As he is in himself, he is En Sof, far beyond human understanding, intuition or description. En Sof reveals himself through the emanation of ten Sefirot, through which all creation comes and to which all worship is directed. Interestingly, the Sefirot are divided into male and female, and into holy and demonic. Humans are the final link in this chain. They influence it by their deeds, good or ill, so that the harmony of all creation depends on human impulses.

Many Jews regarded Kabbalists as dualists, which they denied. So the suspicion in which mainstream Muslims held mystics is true also in Judaism. Similarly, Jewish mystics 'borrowed' concepts from outside the system, from Neo-Platonism and even from Christian theology.

If subverting certain centrally important religious convictions is characteristic of mysticism, so is its willingness to borrow from a wide variety of sources. Zen is a school of Japanese Buddhism. Its name derives from the Chinese *Chan*, a mixture of Buddhism and Taoist nature philosophy. Devotees of Zen use meditation to gain *satori*, an 'enlightenment experience'. For the Rinzai branch of Zen, *koan* is enigmatic or even nonsensical language in meditation; it leads its practitioners away from the intellect towards intuitive insight. Sometimes this is supplemented by *mondo*, questions and answers between masters and disciples, used as riddles to help in meditation. *Satori* may come in a flash; it may be a passing moment or the fullness of *nirvana*. This Zen aspiration for *satori* is a reminder that mystical experiences are not simply between a creature and her creator. Humans who have a non-personal view of Transcendence nevertheless have mystical, intuitive insights that open them up to it and their nature. As a Theravada Buddhist scholar once told me about this experience, 'It is like the unfolding of a flower.'

This eclecticism means that many mystics expect to find traces of ultimate reality outside the religion that they hold. They borrow widely because they intuit that Transcendent reality is universal, at least to the eye that beholds the mystical vision. For example, the Muslim Rumi held that the lamps are different but the light is the same.

festivals and festivities

Although many religions recognise the importance of certain 'spiritual athletes', who inspire others by their very close relationship with ultimate reality, they are also admirably democratic in recognising that ordinary believers can seek and be sought by Transcendence. This often happens through festivities and festivals, and through worship.

The term 'rites of passage' emerged within social anthropology in the early twentieth century, and was touched by that era's conviction of the importance of change and progress. It denotes that human life is marked by change, from conception through to death. In 1909, the Belgian Arnold van Gennep published a study of *Les rites de passage*. In it, he examined rituals from preliterate societies alongside data drawn from the sacred writings of the Hindus, Jews and Christians. His successors have drawn attention to moments in each religion when people move from one point in their life to another. These moments are associated with birth, moments of individual commitment to or enhanced responsibility, and death.

The birth of a child causes rejoicing in most religious communities. Very often there is a naming ceremony, and an event

Adult baptism taking place in a river in Brazil. Full immersion takes place, illustrating the cleansing of both body and soul.

that marks his or her acceptance within the household of faith as well as the social grouping. In some cases these events of naming and acceptance are the same, as in the Christian service of infant baptism. In some cases, the rite is only for male infants. For example, Jewish boys are circumcised on the eighth day. Gifts are often given at such times. Many religions prescribe a ritual of purification for the mother at some point after the birth. In Sikhism, for example, she is given a ritual bath on the thirteenth day.

This element of ritual obtains at other important moments in living and dying; for instance, there is often an event that marks a child's entrance into adulthood. Hindu boys become 'twice-born' in the ceremony of initiation (*upanayana* in Sanskrit, meaning 'drawing near'). The body is invested with the sacred thread (*yajnopavita*) which hangs from the left shoulder to the right hip. The thread is of three cords of nine twisted strands each. Originally this ceremony was for boys of one of the three main castes, but it has come to be restricted to Brahmins. A similar Parsi festival, Naojote, invests a Parsi child, boy or girl, with sacred shirt and thread. The meaning of Naojote is 'new praying' or even 'new birth', so it indicates that thereafter the person can observe religious customs as a full Parsi. When a Jewish boy completes his thirteenth year, he is Bar Mitzvah ('son of the commandment). The following Sabbath he puts on the *tefillin* (cube shaped black leather boxes, attached to the head and arm) and is called up among the men who read from the Hebrew Bible in the synagogue. Among non-Orthodox Jews, increasing numbers of girls who become Bat Mitzvah ('daughter of the commandment') at the age of twelve, also read a portion of scripture at their ceremony, as do boys.

Sometimes, religious festivals are not located in the human life-cycle. Rather, they are linked to a foundational figure or an event of foundational importance in the religion. So, in Christianity the three major feast days are Christmas (the birth of Jesus the Messiah), Easter (his resurrection from the dead) and Pentecost (the downpouring of God's spirit). Jews celebrate a number of festivals, not least Pesach, or Passover, when God 'passed over' the Israelites (Exod. 12:27) but struck down all the other first-born sons in Egypt. As anyone who has ever lived in India can testify, Hindus have a very great number of feasts. An important one is Divali, at the end of the Hindu old year and beginning of the new, in October or November. It is sometimes associated with Lord Rama, or with departed souls, but especially with the goddess of wealth, Lakshmi, wife of Lord Vishnu. Celebrants clean and decorate houses, and wear new clothes. The second day, people stay at home and recite incantations to ward off evil spirits. The third day, people get up early, let off crackers, light fires and entertain friends. In the west Indian state of Gujerat it is an especially important festival. There, businessmen open new account books and write the word Shri for Lakshmi, many times over to bring prosperity.

The word 'feast' is often appropriate. Sometimes these festivals are at the end of a time of fasting: so the Muslim festival of Bakr Eid closes Ramadan, the month of fasting; or the Christian penitential season of Lent concludes with Easter. Even where there is no preliminary period of abstention from food, sex or other human pleasures and exigencies, festivals are quite often times of celebrating. Because festivals punctuate the religious calendar, they are a constant reminder to devotees of the beliefs and practices of their faith. In many countries, religious festivals are public holidays.

In some secularised countries, the meaning of the religious element has been all but forgotten. It was interesting and instructive to hear someone in the British media recently complain that religion had been introduced into too many areas of life, even Christmas.

Yet, precisely because festivals regularly punctuate the year as reminders of a Transcendent dimension to life, they can evoke wonder, awe and even commitment. To strike a personal note, my first religious memory is of a Chinese New Year festival. I was five years old. It was the festival of Lanterns on the fifteenth day of the first month of the Chinese calendar. Then, paper and cloth dragons are lit and carried through the streets as prayer for rain on the spring crops. I was entranced by this extraordinary irruption of mystery into the even tenor of my young life. I wanted to know what was happening and why. Unsurprisingly, my parents could not tell me, since it was not their faith. So I determined to find out for myself, and did, from our Chinese maid. Thus, festivals are a form of teaching and of the evocation of wonder and worship.

worship

What is worship? It is a controversial word, difficult to define. I understand it to indicate two basic attitudes in a religious believer: prayerfulness; and the acknowledgement that its focus, ultimate reality as one describes and experiences it, is worthy of deepest commitment. Members of theistic religions locate God, the gods or a god as the object or objects of their worship. Non-theistic religions have a different goal. For example, Buddhists meditate as a way to enlightenment.

Worship requires constant endeavour, often in the middle of a busy life. Yet, for many believers, it makes all the difference to their lives. Buddhists are inspired by one of the most popular depictions in their religion: the Lord Buddha in meditation, with erect back and crossed legs. He seems serene and imperturbable. Yet that tranquillity and calmness is not a flight from the world for him and his followers, but a means of engaging with it. One Buddhist has said:

> Without having a quiet time or meditation to start my day, I cannot stand. I have to start with it and it is so much joy to do my work alongside Buddhism. I can work more. I can use my time wisely.
> (Harris, 1998, p. 67)

Members of other religions would concur with the sentiment that regular worship sustains, enlightens and liberates the life of the believer. Such worship may be tied to particular festivals. However, most religions commend regular daily prayer and meditation, and it is this obligation which is the subject of this chapter-section.

Let us take Islam as an example, both of a religion where regular worship is seen as a divine command (like Judaism and Sikhism), but also of all religions wherein such worship is hallowed by custom and practice. In offering more detailed commentary on prayer in one religion, the intention is to show how it meshes in with other aspects of human life to reveal Transcendent reality. Each religion does this in its own way, but each sees worship as a demanding and serious experience, permitting humans to engage with ultimate reality in potentially transformative ways.

Formal prayer (*salat*) is obligatory upon every Muslim who is sane, responsible and healthy. Many children begin formal prayer by the age of seven and should certainly have started by ten. Women cannot pray during menstruation or during childbirth and nursing. They are permitted up to ten days of freedom from prayer in the first circumstance, and forty days in the latter.

Prayer is not valid unless certain requirements are met. These requirements emphasise the worshippers' desire to be pure. To this end they dress modestly. A man must cover his body, at least from the navel to the knees. A woman must show only her face, hands and feet. Neither sex must wear transparent clothes. The worshipper must declare the intention that the act is for the purpose of worship and purity. The word *niyyah*, 'intention', is very important in Islam. A well-known tradition states that actions are judged by the intentions associated with them and that doers will receive what they intended. So formal prayer is not just a formality if the prayer is to be effective.

Moreover, the 'minor ablutions' *(wudu)* must be performed, as follows. The person praying declares a sincere intention, and then, usually squatting on haunches and next to a tap or other source of water, washes the hands up to the wrists three times, then rinses out the mouth with water three times, and preferably with a brush. Then the nostrils are cleansed by sniffing water into them three times, and expelling it. Then the face must be washed three times, from the top of the forehead to the bottom of the chin, and from ear to ear; and the right arm, followed by the left, also three times, up to the far end of the elbow. The whole head or any part of it is wiped with a wet hand and the inner sides of the ears with wet forefingers and their outer sides with wet thumbs. The neck is wiped all around with wet hands and the two feet up to the ankles, three times, the right foot first. The *wudu* is then complete. Although it is best done in the order described, it is not forbidden to proceed differently, though the actions recounted must be done. Sometimes, earth, sand, stone or snow can be substituted for plain water. This is usually allowed for reasons of health and availability.

Wudu can be nullified by a number of occurrences. A bodily discharge, such as faeces, urine, flatulence, vomit, the flow of blood or pus voids it. So does falling asleep or taking any intoxicating drug or drink. After such an event, the worshipper must perform *wudu* again.

Wudu is the minor purification. After a major impurity (*janaba*), caused by orgasm, copulation without ejaculation, a wet dream, menstruation, or puerperal discharge after childbirth, and at the end of a nursing mother's confinement period estimated at a maximum of forty days, the major purification (*ghusl*) is obligatory. Many Muslims believe that it is also required on Fridays and on the two festivals at the end of the months of fasting and pilgrimage. The worshipper begins by cleansing the body from sexual fluid, blood or any other impure matter. Then *wudu* is done. Thereafter, a bath is taken, and the body is thoroughly cleansed with water. As with *wudu*, *tayammum* can be performed when no water is available. Many manuals of devotion urge the worshipper to combine such acts of purification with utterances praising God and asking him for guidance.

Until the *hijra*, or emigration, by Muhammad and his followers, from Mecca to Medina in 622, there seem to have been only two daily prayers: sunrise and sunset (Quran 20:130; 17:78). After the *hijra*, the Quran mentions intermediate time or times: 'Glorify God in the evening hour and the morning hour… and in the late afternoon, and when the sun begins to go down.' (30:17f.) It is important to note that these times vary depending on where a Muslim lives. In Saudi Arabia, where Islam began, the time of dawn and dusk varies only slightly throughout the year. In Britain the sun can rise from about 4.30am to 8am, and set from 3pm to 9pm, depending on the month of the year. This controls the times of prayer and varies them considerably.

There are certain times when prayers must not be said: when the sun is rising; when it is at its height; when it is setting; when a woman is menstruating, is in childbirth or is a nursing mother; or when a Muslim is in a state of impurity. Some scholars have argued that the ban on *salat* at sunrise and sunset is related to Hindu worship of the sun. Since Islam believes strongly in *tawhid* (the oneness of God), South Asian Muslims refused to pray during the sun's nadir and zenith lest their prayer should be mistaken for Hindu 'idolatry'.

All prayers should be offered at their due time unless there are compelling reasons otherwise. Muslims are commanded to make up for delayed prayers, except women who are menstruating, are in childbirth or are nursing mothers, and Muslims who are insane or unconscious for some time.

There is no special place where prayers must be said, though some sites are considered unclean and therefore inappropriate, for example, graveyards and lavatories. The mosque, or *masjid*, 'place of bowing down', is a desirable location, where the company of other believers is a stimulus to prayer. In South Asia, custom has determined that women say their prayers at home, not in the mosque, even the Friday congregational prayers, and that habit has transferred to the United Kingdom where most Muslims have their roots in India, Pakistan or Bangladesh. But some Muslims are challenging this habit as unIslamic. In other parts of the Muslim world, women pray in mosques, but in different sections from the men.

When they pray, Muslims face the *qibla*, the direction of prayer towards the *kaba*, the cube-shaped building within the precincts of the Great Mosque of Mecca, built originally by Adam and then rebuilt by Abraham and Ishmael. More precisely, the *qibla* points to the place between the waterspout and the western corner of the *kaba*. Believers pray on a prayer mat, which symbolises space between the believer and the humdrum physical world. A stick or some other object pointing towards Mecca is placed in front. Nobody may pass in between or disturb the devotee.

The *mihrab* or niche in the wall of the mosque indicates the *qibla*. The *mihrab* is often beautifully decorated with calligraphy, tiles and mosaics. Here, craftsmen are encouraged to give full rein to artistic expression in the service of religious fervour. Although music is banned, it has been argued that the *adhan*, 'call to prayer', which is chanted, is a most musical event.

Before each time of prayer, the *adhan* is made by the *muadhdhin* (anglicised as muezzin) from the minaret, one of the towers of a mosque. In Britain and many Western countries, where not all mosques are purpose-built but may be erstwhile shops, factories or private homes, the *adhan* is done from wherever seems appropriate, or, indeed, usually not at all because of legislation banning noise during certain hours of the day and night. (Many Muslims resent this ban when church bells can often be rung without any hindrance.) The first *muadhdhin* was a black African from Ethiopia called Bilal, appointed by Muhammad himself. Muslims often remind themselves of this story to stress the equality of all people before God, which is a central tenet of Islam. The *muadhdhin*, always a man, faces towards Mecca, and begins just before the set time for prayer, except in the case of the morning prayer, when it is usually said in the last sixth of the night so as to give people time to rise and prepare themselves. Nowadays, in many large cities of the Muslim world, and some smaller ones, a recorded tape played through a loudspeaker has replaced the muadhdhin. Not all Muslims approve of this development.

The *adhan* is in Arabic, which translates into English as follows. First the *muadhdhin* says, 'God is greater' four times. Then, 'I testify that there is no other god than God' twice. After this, 'I testify that Muhammad is God's messenger' twice. Then, 'Come to prayer' twice. Thereafter, 'Come to prosperity' twice. Then, 'God is greater' twice. Finally, 'There is no other god than God' once. Just before the dawn prayers, after saying 'Come to prosperity', he adds, 'Prayer is better than sleep' twice. After the utterance 'Come to prosperity', Shia Muslims (who nowadays form about ten per cent of Muslims) interject, 'Come to the best work' at all prayers.

Whether or not the *adhan* is made, the worshippers inaugurate prayer with the *iqama*. It is the same as the *adhan* except that the only phrase said twice is, 'God is greater', and it ends after the statement, 'Come to prosperity'. Then, each devotee says, 'Prayer has begun!' twice.

All five daily prayers consist of a number of ritual prayers and invocations, all of them in Arabic, while standing, bowing, prostrating and sitting. All prayers except for one can be done privately, although Islam encourages congregational prayer. In congregational prayer there is a prayer leader *(imam)*. The *imam* is chosen from among the worshippers. He is respected for his religious learning and piety. In some mosques he is paid to lead prayers and sometimes to teach Arabic and Islam, especially to the children. He stands in front by himself while the congregation line up in straight lines behind him, all facing the *qibla*. A congregation can be any number, even the *imam* and just one other.

The midday prayers on Friday must be said by all Muslim men in a mosque, or some other suitable gathering place such as a home or park. In the Quran (62:9) the believers are commanded, when they hear the call to prayer on Friday, to hurry to the remembrance of God and to cease trading. It is an opportunity to show solidarity with fellow Muslims and to demonstrate that the call of God takes precedence over material and other considerations. A sermon is preached. After these prayers Muslims can return to work, just as they can come from employment to them. There is no Muslim equivalent to the Jewish Sabbath or Christian Sunday, although many Muslim countries take Friday and Saturday as days of rest instead of the Saturday and Sunday common in the West.

In Islam, prayer is a basic element of religion, a foundation pillar. God does not need prayers since he is free of all needs, but human beings need to pray since prayer is a great teacher. The content of the formal prayers, performed regularly, reminds people of the greatness of God, and of the importance of Muhammad and the message that God gave through him. By punctuating the day with prayer, people withdraw from other concerns, however important they may seem, and so assent to God's supreme importance.

There are no sacraments in Islam. But the Quran itself makes much of the signs of God, things which reveal God's presence to the eyes of faith: moon, sun and stars, wind and rain, the creation of people from human semen, and so on (e.g., 30:20–7). So it is not surprising that some scholars have argued that the prayer postures of bowing and prostration are a vivid sign of *Allahu akbar:* 'God is greater' even than humans, his *khalifa*, 'vicegerents' on earth (2: 30–9), who, despite their status, must worship and obey him. Prayer stresses God's will, which Muslim theologians believe is his greatest

*An Islamic worship service. The devout face the prayer niche (*mihrab*) that marks the direction of Mecca, and the* imam *(on the right) leads the service. (Photograph, Joseph Runzo. Reproduced with permission, from* Love, Sex, and Gender in the World Religions. *Oxford, Oneworld, 2000)*

attribute. Extempore prayers are not a central part of *salat* (though *dua*, extempore prayer, can be offered additionally or at any time); *salat* concentrates on God's words, commands, and human responses to them, rather than human requests to God.

In the various religions, the formalities of worship are quite different. This exposition of the central act of a Muslim's worship has aimed to illustrate the seriousness of the enterprise, and the way it links to other aspects of the religion, including (for example) scripture, holy people and holy places.

It is important to emphasise the aesthetic aspect of worship. Outsiders who observe worship may be deeply moved by what they see. For example, to see the serried ranks of Muslims prostrate in prayer can move others to a sense that something serious, transformative and holy is afoot. In a curious way, this can have a compelling, almost missionary quality about it. Similarly, a story is told in the *Russian Primary Chronicle* of how Vladimir, Prince of Kiev, before he became a Christian, sent his followers to various parts of the world to discover the true religion. They tried Islam, and divers forms of Western Christian worship. Finally they journeyed to Constantinople, and here at last, as they attended the Divine Liturgy in the Great Church of the Holy Wisdom [Santa Sophia], they discovered what they desired:

> We knew not whether we were in heaven or on earth, for surely there is no such splendour or beauty anywhere upon earth. We cannot describe it to you: only this we know, that God dwells there among humans, and that their service surpasses the worship of all other places. For we cannot forget that beauty. (Ware, 1993, p.264)

The passage points to two important Eastern Orthodox Christian convictions about worship. First, it expresses on earth the beauty of the spiritual world. Second, worship brings and holds together heaven and earth. It is an icon of the great liturgy in heaven. Of course, the story has legendary elements. Further, it is dismissive of the attempts of other faiths to apprehend and respond to the divine reality in worship. Yet maybe it is not so bad for religious people to want to make others jealous of the beauty and glory of their worship.

spirituality

'Oh that I knew where I might find him', lamented Job, in the midst of devastating sorrow. Job had an advantage over some other humans caught in the midst of meaningless suffering. He wanted to find God, with a great passion. This is not true of all people. Some, in effect, do what his wife advised: curse God, and die. Others live their lives as though there were no Transcendent dimension, either because they do not believe in its existence, or because their lives are focused on other goals.

Job's desire for God made him able to intuit and apprehend the God who spoke to him out of the whirlwind as a phenomenon who made a decisive difference to his life. True, God in the book of Job hardly seems a consistent or likeable or trustworthy figure. Sometimes he is like an indecisive politician, and at other times he resembles an inscrutable despot. It is the genius of the book and its writers that it, they and we can see through these varied, often negative depictions, to a sense of human limitations before the majesty of God who, as Muslims might put it, reveals all of himself that he wills to reveal. Yet there is also the sense by the end of the book, as the English Christian mystic Mother Julian (1342-c.1423) wrote, that 'All is well, and every kind of thing will be well.' This acceptance and even serenity is all the more moving for having been won out of anger and confrontation with God.

Looking at the subject matter of this chapter, it must seem incredible to many secularised or religiously tone-deaf people how mundane things and creatures focus faith's hopes and aspirations for believers: paintings, bread, wine, rivers, wilderness places, particular fallible and wounded humans or even animals, specific writings. To outsiders, these may seem absurd conveyers of divine grace and presence. To the eye of faith, it is precisely the natural that focuses and reveals the supranatural, not always but often enough for faith and hope to flourish. Very often, there is a ritual element to this process of associating a natural phenomenon with ultimate reality: humans need to do certain things or display a committed intention for these things to be charged with the glory of God. Otherwise, even for the believer, they remain simply wood and stone or whatever.

So we have discovered in this chapter that this mundane dimension of existence can be open to a supramundane dimension of ultimate reality, disclosed to faith and, when recognised, obvious and wondrous and more 'real' than this temporal world of sensory experience. Yet it remains profoundly mysterious, even to those caught up in its reality.

We may define spirituality as human responses to alluring Transcendent grace and goodness. It depends on the conviction that there is a Transcendent reality that is revealed through the various subject matter of this chapter. Believers do not keep these in watertight compartments: places, books, people and the rest are in a mutually interactive process, revealing ultimate grace and human response. To that human response, we turn in the next chapter.

the good life

Most humans can differentiate good from evil, right from wrong, even though they often do so rather differently. Many secular people interpret such issues about the good life without any reference to Transcendent reality. They may see certain forms of behaviour as more appropriate than others, as the expression of enlightened self-interest, or as matters of feeling and opinion. Religious people think otherwise. Fundamentally, they believe that humans ought to behave in certain ways because (as Muslims would say) this is the will of God, or (so Buddhists affirm) this is in accordance with *dhamma* (which has a number of meanings, including truth or reality itself).

Since this is a book about religion, we shall examine issues of appropriate human behaviour from a religious standpoint. Faithful humans act out of the primary conviction that Transcendent reality demands a certain life-stance from them. They may also, at a secondary level, act from enlightened self-interest, though often for slightly different reasons than wholly secularised people. They often hope by their actions to achieve blessings in the next life as well as this. They follow prescribed routes in order to acquire these benefits. They believe that humans have a responsibility for the quality of lives that they live. We shall look at these areas in turn. Finally, we shall ask whether we can deduce anything from faithful human behaviour not just about people but also about the nature as well as the commands of Transcendent reality.

life beyond?

Since this life has been short and difficult for most people, many
have believed in a future life or lives where they will find happiness
or some other desirable fulfilment of their aspirations. In chapter 1,
we noted that the great Karl Marx held that hope of a life to come
was the 'opium of the people', the product of wishful thinking by
people who are alienated from social and economic good in this life.
Joe Hill (1879–1914) memorably popularised this Marxist point of
view in his work *The Preacher and the Slave*:

> You will eat (You will eat)
> Bye and bye (Bye and Bye)
> In that glorious land above the sky (Way up high)
> Work and pray (Work and pray)
> Live on hay (Live on hay)
> You'll get pie in the sky when you die (That's a lie.)

How convincing is this critique of religion? We have seen that, from
earliest times, people seem to have believed in a post-mortem
existence. Does this show how deep-rooted an illusion it is, or
suggest rather that it is a universal human intuition about the truth
of something? This is a question to which we must return later in
this section. We can begin to formulate an answer by examining the
variety of views about life after this life that have been held by
members of the world's religions.

　　We can infer from evidence of burial customs from the Upper
Palaeolithic era (*c*.30,000–10,000 BCE) that such life would be a
continuation of life before death. Such beliefs survived into the
Pharaonic period of Egyptian history. In Mesopotamia, the
other early literate society, the 'royal graves' at Ur (*c*.2500 BCE)
indicate that a royal person was attended in death by a retinue of
servants, who were killed at the time of the burial. No doubt the
dead highborn person expected to enjoy in the life beyond the
same life-style to which he had been accustomed in his earthly
existence.

　　This sense of a life beyond life like this one has not been held by
all religions. One of the great early tales about the human condition
is the Epic of Gilgamesh. Tales of him date back to the third

millennium BCE, though they were eventually set down in written form on twelve tablets about 1200 BCE. Although the Epic was told in the same society as that which produced the royal graves, it tells rather of the futility of the human quest for immortality. In it, Gilgamesh is a legendary ruler of Erech, two-thirds god and one-third man. He struggles with a wild beast, Enkidu, sent by the god Anu who is angered by yet fearful of Gilgamesh's arrogance. Gilgamesh and Enkidu become friends and destroy the Bull of Heaven. Enkidu is killed, after which Gilgamesh sets out in search of immortality. He finds his ancestor Ut-Napishtim, who had survived the great flood and become immortal. Ut-Napishtim tells Gilgamesh he cannot attain that state. Gilgamesh vainly disregards him. He dives into the sea to acquire a herb that can make the old young again, but loses it to a serpent as he returns to Erech.

This extraordinarily powerful and moving story shows human courage in challenging the gods, yet human powerlessness to gain the godly prize of immortality. Other cultures portrayed this dilemma in their own ways. The Greek story of Prometheus questioned the hope of immortality as not only vain but nightmarish. He was a demi-god who stole fire from the gods and gave it to humans. Zeus then chained him to a rock where an eagle ate his liver all day. Because he was immortal, it grew again at night. He was bound to the rock in unceasing torment and agony until Heracles rescued him. Interestingly, both Gilgamesh and Prometheus are not fully human. Even their remarkable achievements, though they fall short of attaining what the gods have, are far beyond the hopes of ordinary men to attain.

Other religions have questioned the point of speculating about a life beyond. Many seminal Chinese religious figures were agnostic about the after-life. Kung Fu Tzu (traditionally 551–479 BCE; known in English as Confucius) was a social and ethical reformer who has deeply influenced religious and social life in China and Japan. He refused to speculate on supranatural matters, limiting his attention to this-worldly affairs. When a certain Tzu-lu asked him about his duty to the spirits, Confucius replied, 'When still unable to do your duty to people, how can you do your duty to the spirits?' And inquiring about death, Tzu-lu was told, 'Not yet understanding life, how can you understand death?' (*Analects*, xi.ii). Moreover, original Taoism tended to express the view that humans were fundamentally a part of nature, and so it had little space for a privileged post-mortem existence for them.

Other Chinese views of life after death were less austere. Popular religion came to believe in a realm of the dead comprising ten hells. The Jade Emperor, the supreme deity, assigned control of these to subordinates. After death, each person was judged and punished, and finally made to drink 'the broth of oblivion' so that he forgot his past lives and was then thrown into the crimson river that conveyed him to his new birth. This was greatly elaborated in the popular imagination, not least in the depiction of the hells. Yet Chinese popular religion gave no role to a Creator God in the process of judgement and reincarnation. Rather, human life was seen as a natural, but recurrent, process. It has been argued that the Chinese system of post-mortem judgement was a bureaucratically organised system modelled on centralised imperial government (Brandon, 1967, p.188).

Chinese religion may have appropriated the idea of reincarnation or rebirth from India, through Buddhism. In India, Hinduism came to identify *moksha* (liberation) as the highest goal for humans. This liberates us from a sense of longing for this-worldly things that pass away, and from the repetition of *samsara*, the cycle of births and deaths, to which we are chained. Hindus hold that we do not cease to exist after this present life but are born again in this or another world, with a new body. The universe itself is always existing, but goes through cycles of dissolution and reconstitution; so it is with humans too. One's actions, *karma*, affect how one is reborn. Despite all these rebirths, the *atman*, or self, locates a changeless and eternal human personality. Within the process of *samsara*, the physical body dies but the *atman* continues. Thus *samsara* is not a capricious, hit-or-miss phenomenon. The law of *karma* governs it; the inexorable conviction that actions have reactions and consequences. It could be said that the law of *karma* is the extension into the moral sphere of the physical law of causation.

Buddhism accepted Hindu cyclical beliefs about the process of time and history. However, the Buddha differed from mainstream Hinduism in a number of areas. In his view, all conditioned phenomena, including humans, are impermanent (*annica*); they live in a state of suffering or unsatisfactoriness (*dukkha*), and have no abiding self (*anatta*). This no-self teaching is subtle and easily misunderstood. The Buddha accepted the fact that terms like 'yourself' and 'myself' are a useful way of referring to a particular collection of physical and mental states. But he held that they infer no enduring, tangible and metaphysical Self. There may be continuity within each life and from one life to another, but these features are due to habitual and recurrent *cittas*, 'mind-sets'. Buddhists deal with the issue of how there can be rebirth if there is no enduring self by the teaching of 'dependent origination'. Except for *nirvana*, which is unconditioned, everything comes about from appropriate conditions, and is part of the flux and flow. When someone dies, the energy of his cravings and the impulse of his *karma* finds a new life situation. As the idea of self withers away, a person loses all attachment and attains *nirvana*.

East Asian and South Asian faiths do not quite seem to sustain Marx's critique of religion as an illusory compensation for the economically and socially disadvantaged. Both Confucius and the Buddha refused to speculate overmuch on a life beyond, because this life was the primary arena for human ethical endeavour and philosophical enquiry; and also because unverifiable propositions ought to be avoided as useless speculation. Neither of them denied life after this life. Indeed, the Buddhist view of reality and perhaps even the Confucian cult of the ancestors demand it. But neither Confucius nor the Buddha used recourse to a belief in other lives than this as an easy way out of social, economic or ethical issues. In fact, Chinese and Indian reflections on the continuum of life and death, or lives and deaths, rarely portray future states in a wholly positive light. Certainly, in South Asian views of reality, this life is of fundamental importance in determining whether, or at least how soon, one can escape future ones.

What, however, of the monotheistic faiths of West Asia? After all, Marx was a Jew. Perhaps, then, his sceptical view arose out of his Jewish background. Or perhaps not, since a belief in individual life after death arose late in Jewish scripture. There is no recourse to it in the book of Job. Indeed, in the midst of his sufferings, Job laments in this noble passage:

> For there is hope for a tree,
> If it be cut down, that it will sprout again,
> And that its shoots will not cease.

> Though its roots grow old in the earth,
> And its stump die in the ground,
> Yet at the scent of water it will bud
> And put forth branches like a young plant.
> But man dies, and is laid low;
> Man breathes his last, and where is he?
> As waters fall from a lake,
> And a river wastes away and dries up,
> So man lies down and rises not again;
> Till the heavens are no more he will not awake,
> Or be roused out of his sleep. (14:7–12)

At the end of the book, Job is restored to a privileged continuation of this present life, with another family and greater wealth. The authors did not have recourse to a life beyond where he could be restored to a repentant wife and his innocent and dead children.

The author of the biblical book of Ecclesiastes is often yet wrongly regarded as a cynic. In fact, he expresses the mainstream Jewish view rather movingly: 'The dust returns to the earth as it was, and the spirit returns to God who gave it' (12:7). At most, the ancient Jews believed in a shadowy existence in Sheol, separated from God and from all that made a human being what she essentially is. The author of Psalm 6 declared that: 'In death there is no remembrance of thee; in Sheol who can give thee praise?' (verse 4). For this reason:

> He who is joined with all the living has hope, for a living dog is better than a dead lion. For the living know that they will die, but the dead know nothing, and they have no more reward: but the memory of them is lost. Their love and their hate and their envy have already perished, and they have no more for ever any share in all that is done under the sun. (Eccles. 9:5f.)

When some Jews came to a belief in life after death, there were two strands to their conviction: corporate and individual survival. The first strand was that, despite the tribulations they suffered, the people of Israel would survive. The Northern Kingdom had fallen to the Assyrians in 722/1 BCE; the Babylonians destroyed Solomon's Temple in 587 BCE and deported many Jews into exile. When, under

Antiochus IV Epiphanes (175–163 BCE), the Seleucid dynasty tried to extirpate Judaism, profaning the Temple with a statue of that ruler and provoking the Maccabean rebellion, Jews came rapidly to believe that God would never abandon his people to ruin and extinction. This was expressed in a growing belief in an individual as well as a corporate resurrection. In scripture, both are attested in Daniel, chapter 7 and chapter 12, verses 1 to 4 respectively. This was written at the time of the Maccabean rebellion, when some felt that God must surely reward those martyrs who died for their faith. In the Jewish non-scriptural work, 2 Maccabees, chapter 7 tells of the martyrdom of a mother and her seven sons. She and four of her children testify to their faith that God, who gave them life in the first place, could, if he willed, restore it to them. What sort of life they would be restored to, however, is not clear.

By the end of the scriptural period (the middle of the second century BCE) a small minority of Jews had come to believe in some sort of individual survival after death. Although this process was hastened by a threat to the Jewish people as a whole, another factor would have been the strong sense individual Jews had had for centuries of God's abiding presence and benevolence. We have seen that Job had no recourse to an after-life to justify the goodness of God. Perhaps, however, the logic of his relationship with Yahweh, shared by many of the prophets and psalmists, pointed to the fact that such a firm and enduring dependence upon and even familiarity with the Almighty could not be dissolved by anything, not even by death. Relatively early, it was believed that the prophet Elijah had been taken up to heaven by a whirlwind (2 Kings 2: 1–12). He was a trailblazer for a route that, eventually, others believed they could also take. By the first century BCE, it was strongly attested:

> The souls of the just are in God's hands, and torments shall not touch them. In the eyes of the foolish they seemed to be dead; their departure was reckoned as defeat, and their going from us as disaster. But they are at peace, for though in the sight of men they may be punished, they have a sure hope of immortality; and after a little chastisement they will receive great blessings, because God has tested them and found them worthy to be his. (Wisdom 3:1–5)

That passage is in a post-scriptural book that possibly reflects upon the Maccabean revolt. Yet the biblical period of Jewish history discredits Marx's criticism that religion's grip takes hold by offering supernatural compensations for harsh earthly reality. Jews craved a relationship with God in the here and now, for the most part without any hope that life would continue with him after death.

What of Christian convictions? In the time of Jesus, Pharisees believed in the resurrection, but Sadducees did not. Jesus followed the Pharisees' position on this matter (Mark 12:18–27). He seems to have been as much exercised by a corporate as by an individual resurrection. For example, in the parable of the sheep and the goats, the peoples of the world are divided from each other. Those groups who did good to the needy go to eternal life but those who failed to do so enter eternal punishment (Matt. 25:31–46). Although this passage is often preached on as if it were about individual judgement, that is not its thrust.

Modern Western people often misjudge the distinction between individual and society in many other societies. There, human beings have their identity largely shaped by societal conventions. Society, often sanctioned by religious teaching, governs whom individuals can marry, what they can wear, and many details of daily life. In the West, the emphasis upon individual libertarianism means that many people find it difficult to understand cultures where customs are quite different. Yet individuals also matter in non-Western societies. We explored in chapter 1 how Jesus' parable of the Prodigal Son casts light on, but is also explicable within, the customs and habits of first-century Mediterranean societal practices. Yet withal, the story is about individuals struggling to understand human sin and divine grace.

Therefore, Westerners must not overemphasise the importance of either individual or society when they look beyond their own cultural settings. Early Christians picked up the Jewish belief in both a communal and an individual resurrection. Equally, Christians shared with Jews the conviction that religion was meaningful for this life as well as holding out the promise of another one. The greater emphasis in Christianity than in Judaism upon a future existence is probably explained by the fact that it came into being towards the beginning of the period when considerable numbers of Jews had come to believe in life after death.

The apostle Paul who, as a Pharisee, believed in the resurrection (Acts 23:6), saw the raising by God of Jesus from death as the beginning of the harvest of the resurrection of all things (1 Cor. 15). This clearly had social as well as individual connotations. He argues that all die in Adam, the representative sinful human, but all are raised in Christ, the representative obedient and redeemed human. This vision of a universal resurrection of all humans as perfected beings is not simply 'pie in the sky'. In this life, Christians are to be the body of Christ, aiming at exercising ministries for the common good, especially through love (1 Cor. 11–13).

Although its teaching about life after death is strongly individualistic, Islam lays great stress on an *umma* or community obedient to God in this life. So here again, belief in an after-life cannot simply be dismissed as providing heavenly compensation for earthly pain and brutality. Muslims believe in an individual resurrection. On the last day, there will be trumpet blasts (Quran 39:68). God will appear as the only eternal being: 'Everything will perish but his face.' (28:88). A person's deeds will be weighed in the scales (42:17). Evildoers will go to hell, a terrifying place of scorching fire (88:1–7). Yet, according to most Muslims, most Muslims will eventually enter Paradise because 'whoever has done an atom's weight of good will see it' (99:8). Paradise is most usually described as a garden; this marks a heavenly contrast to the earthly desert area of Arabia where the Quran was revealed.

Are not these pictures of heaven and hell (and also limbo, which the Quran also describes) an offence to right-minded people? Not only Islam but also many other religions of the world describe the great and barbaric pains of those in hell. Although such language is often developed in grotesque and even sadistic ways in the fevered imagination of some devotees, the notion of the severe punishment of malefactors is present at the heart of many religions. One explanation is that they are not to be taken literally. Many religious people who have been influenced by the ideas of Western modernity have followed this route. The Indian Muslim biographer of Muhammad, Syed Ameer Ali (1849–1928), wrote that 'the idea of eternal punishment is repellent to Islam... [God] is withal pitiful and compassionate... Whatever punishment man undergoes here or hereafter is only for purifying or fitting him to enter that state of perfection which will bring him "nigh unto God".' Nevertheless,

Ameer Ali had long believed that the concept of punishment could be defended, not so much because it was true as because it was socially expedient. He wrote that: 'We must bear in mind that these ideas have furnished to the moral teachers of the world, the most powerful instruments for influencing the conduct of individuals and nations... virtue for its own sake, can only be grasped by minds of superior development; – for the average intellect, and for the uneducated, sanctions more or less comprehensible will always be necessary.' Ameer Ali's interpretation of the Quranic evidence about life after death was idiosyncratic. Indeed, although he believed that Muhammad's description of the hereafter was 'word-paintings', he admitted that the largest number of Muslims have believed in their 'literal fulfilment'. (Forward, 1999, p.39f.)

Although Ameer Ali's was an eccentric interpretation, he has not been alone in arguing that the language of heaven and hell is not literal but mythic. Indeed, since few if any people have ever died and returned to tell us their tales, he has a point. Perhaps this point is better illustrated by a foundational religious figure like Confucius. His agnosticism about life after this life was not due to a lack of belief that there is more to life than meets the eye. Rather, he pointed to this life as the arena for faithfulness and obedience, for goodness and charity. The depictions of heaven and hell also make this point. What we do here matters in terms of its consequences hereafter. Religion therefore cannot simply be dismissed as compensation. Such a passive view ignores the moral and faithful endeavours that belief in life after this life requires from those who believe in it.

There is, of course, a strong element of enlightened self-interest in acting appropriately in order to attain *nirvana* or *moksha*, or to reach heaven's joys. Religious people who believe in a personal God certainly worship God with a view to benefiting from such a relationship. Yet some such worshippers also display a sense that relating to the deity cannot simply be reduced to transactional matters.

In chapter 3, we noted the selfless devotion to God of the early Muslim woman mystic, Rabia al-Adawiyya. Similarly, a hymn attributed to Francis Xavier (d.1552 CE), the founder of the Roman Catholic Jesuit order, emphasises the love of God for its own sake:

My God, I love Thee – not because
I hope for heaven thereby,
Nor yet because who love Thee not
Are lost eternally

Then why, O blessèd Jesus Christ,
Should I not love Thee well?
Not for the sake of winning heaven,
Or of escaping hell;

Not with the hope of gaining aught;
Not seeking a reward;
But as Thyself has lovèd me,
O ever-loving Lord.

Neither Rabia nor Francis Xavier (if it were he) was spurning the hope of heaven. They were poets and mystics, accepting the gift but loving the giver for more than the gift. Similar sentiments could be quoted from many theists: for example, from God-intoxicated Hindus from the *bhakti* tradition; from members of African traditional faiths and other first peoples.

Sometimes similar prayers express a preference for the giver rather than the gift in rather a different way. A prayer from a tribe of Northern Bengal runs:

If I ask him for a gift, he will give it to me, and then I shall have to go away. But I don't want to go away. Give me no gift – give me thyself. I want to be with thee, my beloved.

Such sentiments express a devotion to God that is intended as a worthy and analogous response to what is believed to be God's indestructible love for human devotees.

The lack of a creator God in many South and East Asian religions (elsewhere too) does not mean that such devotion is not found there, at a popular level. Geoffrey Parrinder has consistently claimed that Buddhism has become a religion because its followers, in practice if not in theory, worship God, the gods, the Buddha or some other saviour-type figure. (So, analogously, Jainism, Confucianism and other religions who have no creator God are also religions in Parrinder's sense that they offer worship to a foundational figure.) In *An Introduction to Asian Religions* (1957) he argued that even the austere form of Theravada Buddhism can be designated as a religion because of the devotion given to the Buddha:

> It can be said that the Buddha himself represents for the faithful an ultimate religious symbol. The devotion that is lavished on the Buddha, in Hinayana [more properly, Theravada] as well as Mahayana countries, the innumerable statues which are the work of loving craftsmen, the constant offerings, the bowings and prayers, all point to a deep religious experience. It is true that in theory the Buddha is an example, and that the task of the faithful is the 'Imitation of Buddha', but imitation turns to adoration and religious experience. (p.84)

In *Avatar and Incarnation* (1970), Parrinder asserted that 'the Buddha is a substitute-deity'. He recognised that:

> There are some writers who object that not only is the Mahayanist glorification [of the Buddha] a departure from original Buddhism, but that the notion of a Buddha saving men is also an intrusion. Such objections are heard in the western world and on the fringes of Buddhism, from westernized Japanese or Ceylonese. The Buddha is represented as a humanist, a Socratic, almost a scientific figure, and he is not called Saviour except in the sense that he discovered and showed the path to liberation. But in all traditional schools and scriptures the Buddha is regarded as supreme, he has numinous qualities, and not only his teaching but his presence and protection are sought, daily, and in the cult of relics and holy places. (p.248)

Parrinder is well aware that his 'view of the Buddha as a "functional deity" is controversial, but it is based both on observation, in Burma and Japan, and on reading the texts'. It has the merit of observing what many Buddhists do, and of taking into account the fact that many strands of Buddhism are not atheistic in the strict sense that there are no gods.

The problem with Parrinder's description of the Buddha as a 'functional deity' is that it scans the evidence from an alien viewpoint. In Buddhism the Buddha shows the way to the cessation of human suffering and is the embodiment of wisdom and compassion; he is therefore the focus of reverence which theists would naturally believe appropriate only for God. But he is only a human being. Nevertheless, Parrinder has detected a very important point. There does seem to be a common human need to offer reverence or even worship in the face of life's mysteries. Yet Buddhist scholars have cogently argued that, even at a popular level, ordinary Buddhists can distinguish between reverence and worship. The Buddha is reverenced for the path towards liberation that he has shown humans. Bodhisattvas and gods may also be reverenced for certain particular boons they can bestow. But this is not the worship of an Almighty Creator God. (Forward, 1998a, pp.141–144)

So most human beings, except eccentrically in the modern and post-modern West, seem to have an innate disposition to respond to mystery in reverence or worship. That disposition establishes and sustains a relationship with ultimate reality, sometimes of a remarkable degree.

In what state do humans approach and engage with Transcendence? Broadly speaking, there is a distinction between Semitic (West Asian) and South and East Asian perceptions. West Asian religions define their adherents as disobedient to or forgetful of a Creator God. In South and East Asian religions, devotees are regarded as ignorant of the nature of ultimate reality. This is, of course, a useful but rather unrefined distinction. Obviously, Jains may be wicked and Zoroastrians can be unaware of important matters!

It is worth exploring this distinction between disobedience and ignorance a little. In the next section, we shall see that Sunni Muslims set out to follow the straight path of the *Sharia*, religious law that defines how they can faithfully follow God's will. The rationale for this is that humans are often forgetful of God's bounty, and need constant reminders of it. Humans easily fall into disobedience. In Hinduism, people are regarded as victims of ignorance (*avidya*; literally, 'not-knowing'). In one Hindu school of thought, we humans impose upon our real self (*atman*) the qualities of our limited human bodies. In fact, the *atman* (in this particular interpretation) is identifiable with *brahman*, the self in its cosmic and universal nature as the reality of all existence. The end of ignorance is in understanding this identification and acting accordingly. This is, in summary, the approach of the great

Shankara (*c.*788–820 CE). Other Hindu schools of philosophical thought interpret the nature of *atman* and *brahman* differently, and therefore differ about how ignorance can be overcome. This illustrates the great variety of opinion within and also between religions about the human condition.

One more example may be drawn from certain Muslim criticisms of Christianity. Certain forms of Christianity portray human disobedience as a cosmic tragedy, the endless human repetition of Adam's initial disobedience from which humanity can only be freed by the atoning sacrifice of Jesus Christ upon the cross. This is, if you like, Christianity's equivalent of Hindu's *samsara*, the endless chain of misery from which people must be freed. To Muslims (and to quite a few Christians), this seems an overstatement of human wrongdoing (see, for example: Forward; 1999, p.66f.). Nevertheless, despite the differences between these perceptions, Muslims and Christians (Jews and Zoroastrians too), though they recognise human ignorance of ultimate reality, characteristically emphasise human disobedience. Hindus and Buddhists (Jains and Sikhs too) are well aware of people's disobedience, but are more essentially concerned with their ignorance.

Religious people believe that there is more to life than meets the eye. Therefore, it ought not to be surprising that they are open, not only to Transcendent grace and goodness but also to the possibility that such ultimate reality is not confined to the apprehension of the physical senses or to this life only. Even so, we have noted wide responses to the nature and importance of life after this life, and to the human condition that life after life seeks to address and redress. Cynics would say that this proliferation of views confirms the incoherence and improbability of this human hope. Rather, it may be that the very universality of such views is impressive evidence for the thesis that there is substance in them. On this view, these views are so pluriform because they are clothed in variant cultural and linguistic garments.

For many religious people, a belief in life after this life does not diminish this life's importance. In fact, what we do here seriously impacts upon our future hope. So, how are humans to obey the way the world works, whether interpreted as the will of a Creator God and so to attain paradisal joys, or working with and not against the grain of *samsara* so as to achieve *moksha* or *nirvana*?

the way through dusty death

We live at a time of enormous human achievement. Within the lifetime of many contemporary people, men have climbed Mount Everest and landed on the moon. The great achievements of the future, not least planetary exploration, may be for the few. Yet there is one mystery that faces us all: the enigma of death. Perhaps we could call it life's last great adventure.

That speculative endeavour may be upon us sooner than we care to think. The world has not been the same since 6 August 1945, when an atomic bomb fell on Hiroshima, Japan, killing over a quarter of the city's inhabitants immediately. Many more died painfully in months and years to come. The bomb had been tested in the desert of New Mexico on 16 July. When Dr Robert Oppenheimer, the leader of the scientists who made the bomb, saw the resulting mushroom cloud, he quoted the Lord Krishna's words from the Bhagavad Gita: 'I am become Death, the shatterer of worlds.' On 21 July 1969, another American, Neil Armstrong, also quoted from scripture, this time the Hebrew Bible, when he set foot on the moon: 'In the beginning, God created the heavens and the earth.'

So religion is closely tied in with human behaviour and achievement. It can cause the flourishing of humane values, but has also been used to justify or comment upon appalling deeds, even genocide. In this section, we shall examine certain trends in religions that promote and sustain ethical endeavours. Because we live in a world over which the threat of nuclear annihilation hangs, we shall particularly ponder whether there is any common ethical core to religions that would promote humane values in the contemporary world.

Some religions have made an ethical system central to their *raison d'être*. The most notable example is Confucianism. Confucius advocated filial piety and ancestor rites. He was not a sceptic, though we have seen that he was cautious about claiming too much knowledge about matters beyond our mundane existence. His sense of mission derived from *Tien*, heaven, a power that he felt had moral authority. Confucius promoted a number of virtues that marked him as an outstanding teacher in a climate of political instability and the often brutal use of power. They included *jen* (goodness, benevolence) and *shu* (reciprocity). He appropriated the term *chun tzu*, 'son of a noble', to refer to a person of moral character, whatever his birth. Early Confucian thought was an almost intuitive process of responding harmoniously to matters with one's *te* (moral power, derived from heaven). All relationships derive from the family: filial piety and brotherly affection are the model for good government. This has encouraged extreme deference in Chinese society. No wonder its Marxist phase has made of Mao and others a personality cult.

Even so, Confucianism has been criticised by other important teachings. Mo Ti (470–391 BCE) questioned any ethical position or institution that did not benefit the masses. So he condemned warfare in general and military expansionism in particular, questioned many ancient rites and traditions, and forsook filial piety for universal love (*chien ai*). Taoism also provided an ethical alternative to Confucian values. In origin, this was anti-authoritarian and almost anarchic. The sage must model himself on the nameless Tao, 'eternal principle', in self-effacement and self-emptying. The Tao became the unity under the plurality of the universe, the indefinable principle of all things. It is a mystical concept that led devotees to search for harmony with it, through magic and ascetic practices. The *Chuang Tzu* is a book of thirty-three chapters, said to date to the fourth century BCE and to be the work of a man of the same name. It looks now to have been written over a much longer period of time by a number of people. It rejects absolute claims, even Confucian appeals to universal principles. It follows a natural sense of morality, innate to the moral do-er; this combines situational adaptability with referral to a higher perspective that issues either from *Tien* (heaven) or *te* (virtue). Later Chinese thought was deeply influenced by other viewpoints, not least Buddhist insights.

If aspects of Chinese religion show one extreme, in which ethics is central to religion, at the other end of the spectrum there are certain religious manifestations that show an indifference to morality. The Christian apostle Paul may have had to deal with converts who misunderstood his teaching about sin and grace to mean that the more you sinned, the more God was gracious (Rom. 6:1)! He strenuously attempted to disabuse them of this false conviction.

Tantric Hinduism, a heterodox movement frowned upon by many Hindus, relies on texts from the eighth and ninth centuries. It is surrounded by an aura of mystery and secrecy, because certain rituals violate normal morality and Hindu custom. These texts are mainly dialogues between the god Shiva and his Shakti (wife) called Devi or Durga. They deal with five subjects: creation, destruction, worship, superhuman powers, and union. Central to Tantric Hinduism is the energy of the female Shakti. Each Shakti has a kindly and fierce, white and black, nature and practitioners are similarly divided into right-hand and left-hand worshippers. The latter especially seek for magical and sexual powers through the five Ms. Though these are forbidden things, they are holy and form the substance of certain Tantric rites. They translate into English as: wine, meat, fish, hand gestures, and sexual union. Despite the secrecy surrounding aspects of Tantricism, it is easy to get hold of texts about the forbidden rituals, and equally easy to be shocked by them. But this would be to miss at least two important points. First, this is an example of how uneasily yet insightfully many religions deal with the feminine. Shakti power is depicted as wild, uncontrollable, energising, a cosmic force. This shows both how astute male Tantric practitioners were about the power of the female, yet also how they attempted to control and harness it so that they could manipulate rather than be destroyed by it. Secondly, Tantricism possibly fulfils a role in Hinduism not unlike the figure of Seth did in ancient Egyptian religion. In chapter 2 we saw how Seth was not utterly cast out of the world by the victorious Horus, but at least for a time was retained within it as the destructive and undisciplined power standing alongside the forces of order. Religion is about wild and dark and uncontrollable forces, not just about goodness, moderation and thoughtfulness. Indeed, the good life is often depicted even in mainstream religion as an overcoming of the force of evil. The Confucian ethical ideal is rather too formal to stand as exemplary of how religions normally understand their central concerns, just as Seth and practitioners of Tantricism illustrate real concerns, though ones not quite at the centre of most religious endeavours.

In many religions, moral issues are neither absolutely central nor marginal but derive much more clearly from either belief in a personal God or else from a Transcendental view of how the world really works, so that one must not go against its grain. Some such religions tie moral achievement in to a cyclical view of time, with many births. Hinduism, Buddhism and some other religions tie *karma* ('action'; and the fruit of action) into a hierarchy of life forms. If I perform badly in this life, I might become a monkey or a mosquito in a future existence. Or else I can move upwards through (in Hinduism's case) the caste system and eventually achieve *moksha*. Some primal religions have a belief in the transmigration of souls, but it is not linked to deeds.

Pagans are followers of what literally means the religion of the countryside, the primal religion of a country as it has either survived into the present age or been recovered by modern people. Paganism is a religion that reverences and celebrates nature, with festivals, that vary from place to place, based on the agricultural, solar and lunar calendars. In Europe, adherents regard this as 'the old religion', predating Christianity which has 'borrowed' certain practices from it. (For example, Christmas Day in the Northern Hemisphere is around the time of the winter solstice, when pagans celebrate the rebirth of the world from the womb of the Mother Goddess.) Paganism is a far from unified phenomenon. However, most pagans believe in a series of lives but do not hold that karmically burdened souls return as lesser beings than humans. For them, all life is equal. Many pagans believe that all life is part of the Great Spirit and therefore has an animating soul. Humans cannot claim to be more significant than cats and tigers or even rocks and stones; though they have more knowledge about their situation. The purpose of transmigration is for the soul to evolve, experiencing many panoramas and possibilities. There is no *moksha* or *nirvana*. Instead, there is the everlasting joy of being and learning. This means that the ethical stance of many modern pagans is that of moral relativism coupled with a strong streak of individualism and libertarianism. No wonder then that paganism appeals to marginalised and even eccentric (in the sense of 'outside the centre') people. Women hold positions of responsibility (sometimes as priestesses or witches), and pagans are indifferent about issues of sexual orientation.

In religions where there is a clear notion of reincarnation as a means of ethical improvement, what constitutes the good over and against the evil is not always clear-cut. The *Jina*s, twenty-four

Seventeenth-century piece of artwork depicting Jain pandits of the Shvetambara school presenting an edict to their guru prohibiting the slaughter of animals during the Paryushana festival.

'conquerors' of this age, taught Jainism. The first lived millions of years ago. The last was Mahavira, who died c.468 BCE. Jains teach non-violence (*ahimsa*). Jain temples often have the text 'Non-violence is the highest religion'. Jains do not eat meat or certain vegetables, out of respect for all living things. They do not follow pursuits like hunting, farming or professions that lead them to take up arms. Some Jain monks and nuns (and occasionally even lay people) wear cloth over their mouths and noses so as to avoid breathing in small insects. Such Jains often also brush the ground in front of them to avoid stepping on a living thing.

Once, I went to the home of a distinguished Jain family in Britain in whose bathroom was a bottle of bleach. Its makers tell us that it kills all known household germs. I was amused and intrigued. Here is an example of the need to accommodate one's beliefs to the modern world. Many Jains now see their religion as commending veganism and pacifism. It has not always been thus. Some would see this as a trivial reductionism of the faith. But many more would interpret this as an appropriate way of contextualising faith in the contemporary world. Until recently, Jains and Hindus alike could scarcely believe that religion could be lived out beyond the *kala pani*, the 'black waters' bearing people away from the holy land of India. Now, the South Asian Diaspora to other parts of the world has led many thoughtful believers to ask how (not, as their grandparents would have asked, whether) principles rooted in rural, premodern Asia can be adapted to (for example) urban, post-modern Chicago, Durban or London.

The great Mahatma Gandhi (1869–1948), who came from a Jain-influenced area of Western India, favoured non-violent resistance (*satyagraha*) against British imperial rule in India. His favourite text was the Bhagavad Gita. This is the sixth book of a great epic poem, the Mahabharata, the longest poem of all. It is a collection of legend, myth, theology, ethical and philosophical teaching. The central theme is the contest for power between the Kuru family and their cousins the Pandus. The blind Kuru King Dhritarashtra had nominated the Pandu Yudhishthira as his successor. But Dhritarashtra's jealous son drove Yudhishthira (who also brought about his own downfall by gambling) and his brothers into forest exile. Twelve years later the Pandu brothers fought for the kingdom and, after much bloodshed, gained it.

In the Gita, the great God Krishna acts as charioteer to the third brother, Arjuna. The scenario opens on the plain of Kurukshetra, outside modern Delhi. When Arjuna sees that the opposing forces contain many relatives, he is horrified. He says he would sooner be killed than kill. Krishna responds with a number of reasons for fighting in particular and for all actions in general. The most important is that the true soul is immortal, 'it does not kill or be killed'. An important part of the discussion centres on *dharma*, fulfilling one's 'duty'. It is Arjuna's duty as a warrior to fight. Since the soul is immortal, he must do his duty as detached action without the seeking of reward. The most extraordinary passage of the Gita is chapter 11, when Arjuna receives a divine eye to see the transcendent body of Krishna. His hair stands on end as the God appears in majestic form and is hailed as Vishnu. Krishna shows him grace and comforts him.

This extraordinary work is about human suffering and evil, human duty, divine power and love. At first blush, it seems odd that Gandhi should have been inspired by a work that describes internecine warfare. Yet it also describes divine love and human duty. It is a work that has been interpreted in fascinatingly different ways. Many scholars have seen it as a central text for theistic Hinduism, celebrating *bhakti*, loving devotion to a personal god. Others have seen it more philosophically, encouraging readers to interpret it as a monistic text, pointing to the fundamental oneness of all things and beings.

Ethically, the Bhagavad Gita is a powerful and disturbing work. Not many texts about a battle are used by iconic figures who are associated with non-violence! Although Gandhi himself was a pacifist, the scripture is more multifaceted than his interpretation of it was. No wonder that Oppenheimer quoted from chapter 11 of the Gita on observing the first powerful nuclear detonation. Part of that passage, describing Krishna's revelation to Arjuna as sovereign God, runs:

> If ever in the sky there comes
> the brilliance of a thousand suns
> that might resemble as a whole
> the brilliance of that mighty soul. (Parrinder, 1996, p.73)

Thus, religions provide resources for the construction of the good life, or the evil one. But these resources often prove less unvaried and consistent, more multivalent, than people recognise. One relatively clear message of the Gita is the need to perform one's *dharma*. So a warrior like Arjuna can and must do so, confident that the eternal soul never dies. Better that he kill a kinsman out of duty, than to shirk his obligation as a warrior.

The caste system provided Hindus for centuries with the means of understanding what they must do. They might be warriors, priests, traders, farmers or whatever. The good life was to be achieved by faithfully fulfilling one's duty in the life situation in which one found oneself. Such faithfulness would build up good *karma* so that one's position improved in further lives. Caste boundaries have been preserved through marriage restrictions. Marriages have traditionally been arranged so as to preserve this. Of course, there have always been exceptions, some more accepted than others. In modern India, and in the Hindu Diaspora, this is breaking down to some extent. Yet there is also much resistance to change. Further, the emphasis upon performing one's duty in a disinterested way remains a powerful ideal for many modern Hindus.

The Buddha was against the caste system. Like other indigenous South Asian religions, Buddhism works with hierarchical and developmental notions of ethical endeavour but would regard the caste system as both oppressive and implying too stable and everlasting a view of existence. What counts as good in Buddhism is the overcoming of suffering or liberation from views and deeds that bind one to the chain of *samsara*. This means that, although Buddhism has a view of reality as in flux, and is therefore suspicious of making references to individuals and societies that imply their permanence, many Buddhists attempt to help others as well as themselves achieve *nirvana*. Meditation is not simply an individual matter but can rectify our wrong thoughts, words and deeds. These have important consequences in terms of our understanding of and dealing with others. The Buddha said about the effect of *karma*, 'Pull yourself out as an elephant from the mud.' In Theravada Buddhism, the Buddha is regarded as a great example, though in Mahayana Buddhism there is belief in a Buddha nature as the universal cosmic principle. Mahayana holds that we should seek to free others from suffering. The ideal is the Boddhisatva, a person who strives for enlightenment so that he can help others to become enlightened too.

There are four Buddhist heavenly states of mind and methods of meditation: love; compassion; joy; and serenity. Perhaps the most important is the second, *karuna* or compassion, which enables devotees to identify themselves with the suffering of others.

Buddhism has spread over much of the world. It soon left India, the land of its birth, where it almost died out, but rooted itself in Sri Lanka and throughout East Asia. Nowadays, Buddhism has exercised a wide influence in the West, where many people of Jewish or Christian origin prefer its different analysis of the human predicament. The Friends of the Western Buddhist order was founded in England in 1967, and consciously strives to make the practice of Buddhism relevant to the West. It has founded the Karuna Trust, working to alleviate suffering among Buddhists in India, many of whom are recent converts from outcaste Hindus.

Religions of West Asia are among those that traditionally have no belief in *samsara* or the transmigration of souls. Judaism was formed from the conviction that the unnameable personal God had called them as a people. Under the leadership of Moses, he led them out of the iron furnace of Egypt, where they had been enslaved and persecuted. At Sinai, they were established as his people, through covenant and *Torah*. Torah is the whole of Jewish law, the continuing revelation of God. It is a gift from God to his people of Israel.

The traditional view is that God gave Written Torah (the first five books of the Hebrew Bible) to Moses. He also gave Oral Torah, a detailed elaboration of the laws and doctrines contained in Written Torah (including the rest of the Hebrew Bible) and also the Mishnah, the Talmud and all the later teachings of Jewish sages. Although this has been questioned by modern reconstructions of Judaism since the 1840s, the centrality of Torah is characteristic of most Jewish groups.

In Judaism, ethics is part of religion. Law and ethics are interdependent but not identical. Torah prescribes for parts of life which modern Western people often assume should be nothing to do with religion. So the fact that a Jew is a Jew (in Orthodox belief) if his or her mother is a Jew, places limits on marriage. Jews eat Kosher ('fit' or 'suitable') food. For example, they cannot eat meat with milk; pork; or a number of other foods. Sometimes, modern Jews argue (for example) that pork goes off quickly in hot countries, hence the reason for not eating it. Yet a more traditional argument is that human reasoning in this area is irrelevant: humans should simply obey God's law.

Because the law is God's gift, following it is not a burden but a pleasure. Psalm 119 expresses this well: 'Oh, how I love thy law (Torah)! It is my meditation all the day' (verse 97). Torah provides a boundary within which Jewish life can flourish. Observing it enables devotees to live the life that God requires. In a wider sense, Torah is for humankind. The Noahide Laws provide seven laws given to Noah, the father of humankind, after the flood. They include the prohibition of idolatry, blasphemy, murder, robbery, adultery and incest, and the need to establish a proper system of justice. If the Gentiles obey these laws, they have a share in the life of the world to come. Furthermore, the Torah provides rules by which Jews are to treat strangers and aliens in their land with justice. Moreover, the law is intended to lay down guidelines for dealing appropriately with the environment. For example, the biblical book of Leviticus (25:2–4) urges a rest in the seventh year for the land from sowing and reaping. Thus it is refreshed and can regain its vigour.

Muslims also follow religious law. About ninety per cent of Muslims are Sunni, following the *sunna* or 'trodden path' laid down by the Prophet Muhammad. They believe that the Sharia (Muslim religious law) was not an innovative development over the two centuries after the Prophet's death before it was finally set in place. Rather, it was the logical drawing out of what was essentially in place upon his death. A limited diversity is permitted within the broad framework of Sunni Islam: four law schools exist, and every Sunni Muslim belongs to one of them. Yet an overarching unity binds together Sunni Muslims, from California to Indonesia. Laws about, for example, what one can wear and eat, how to worship, and whom one may marry, are similar wherever one travels in the *dar al-Islam* ('the household of Islam', areas in which the majority of people are subject to the divine law). Although many aspects of Muslim law are similar to Jewish, there are differences. Many Muslims describe their community as the 'middle way' between what they regard as the too rigid formalism of Judaism and the laxity of Christianity. As with Jewish Torah, Muslim law instructs Muslims to treat their environment with respect. Some modern Muslims interpret the Quran 55:7, which tells that 'God has lifted the heavens up high, and has set up the balance (*mizan*)', to mean that the world is delicately balanced by God. Only if people preserve that balance by using science and technology aright will they properly obey God's will. Moreover, the law carefully describes the appropriate use of natural resources like land and water, so as to allow appropriate access to them by humans, but also their responsibility for right usage of them.

Of course, it is not just Jews and Muslims who are committed to care for nature and the environment. Most religions have much to say about respect for the earth, even if these are not always shaped by religious law but instead by custom, practice and other factors. In particular, many of the first peoples of the earth live in fragile environments and are the first to suffer from the degrading of the ecosystem by environmental pollution. They often live close to the land, and have a knowledge of, for example, medicinal plants that some Western doctors are now beginning to take seriously. There is a strong sense among many such people that the land is only to be used, not owned, and that to abuse it would destroy the delicate balance between humans, the rest of creation and the spirit world.

The Christian attitude towards religious law is rather more ambivalent than that of Jews and Muslims. Many Protestants interpret the Apostle Paul as someone who not only rejected but also condemned Torah observance as misplaced. Some go further and picture Jesus as the destroyer of Jewish legalism. This is a misleading overemphasis of what Jesus did, and a trivialisation (as we have just seen) of the importance of Torah for Jews. The Gospel of Matthew has Jesus say:

> Think not that I have come to abolish the law and the prophets; I have come not to abolish them but to fulfil them. For truly, I say to you, till earth and heaven pass away, not an iota, not a dot, will pass from the law until all is accomplished. (5:17f.)

This may be hyperbole but it is not irony, exaggeration but not derision. Like all Jews, Jesus, and Paul after him, would have seen Torah as a gift from God. Also like all Jews, they would have interpreted it, and argued over its interpretation with others.

Both Jesus and Paul differed from many first century Jews in counting as clean what others counted as unclean, whether certain sorts of food or even Gentiles. Jesus had some particularly fierce words to say about food; that nothing can defile a person by what she eats (Mark 7). Arguably, this attitude towards the potential purity of everyone accounted for the success of the early Christians as they took a form of Jewish ethical monotheism out into the pagan world of the Roman Empire.

The early Christians were urged to love each other (1 Cor. 13). Perhaps the most famous teaching of Jesus is his Sermon on the Mount (Matt. 5–7). Matthew presents Jesus as the new Moses. This 'Sermon' is one of five blocks of ethical teaching in that Gospel, recalling the heart of Torah, the five books of Moses at the beginning of the Hebrew Bible. For Matthew and Paul, Jesus fulfilled the law as the embodiment of God's love (Gal. 5:14). Theirs was certainly a radical reinterpretation of Jewish law, but in his own mind Paul remained a Pharisee (Acts 23:6), with a Pharisee's love of interpreting the Torah. So it is best to interpret fulfilment, not as love replacing the law, but as being the heart of the law. This is almost exactly the position that Rabbi Hillel had come to a little before the time of Jesus, as we shall see later in this chapter.

Nevertheless, Christians have interpreted the need to love God and love neighbour rather differently from their Jewish and Muslim monotheistic 'cousins'. Characteristically, they look to the ethical teaching of Jesus as the source of inspiration for the good life. At times, certain Christians have constructed 'systems' or ways by which they can appropriate and share that love. For example, monks and nuns, and also mystics, have lived by rules of life and worship that enable them to encounter God and live out the life of Jesus. Many Christians have been brought up on the Ten Commandments, read out weekly in some Christian services. More notably, the beatitudes at the beginning of the Sermon on the Mount provide inspiration rather than specific rules by which Christians attempt to live their lives.

the moving finger?

The Moving Finger writes; and having writ,
Moves on: nor all thy Piety nor Wit
Shall lure it back to cancel half a Line,
Nor all thy tears wash out a Word of it.

Are human beings in a position to respond freely to how things really are, or are they constrained by forces beyond their control? These words are from Edward Fitzgerald's nineteenth-century paraphrase (rather than translation) of the *Rubaiyat* of Omar Khayyam. To some extent, Fitzgerald imposed his own Christian fatalistic viewpoint on this minor work of a medieval Muslim.

Monotheistic religions often seem to promote fatalism over free will, at least in some of their forms. The Hebrew Bible records the failure of Jews to live up to their side of the covenant obligations with God. Christianity has a strong sense of human sin and disobedience, and Islam an equally definite recognition of human forgetfulness of God's will. So it seems logical that these religions would stress God's control of events rather than human capacity ultimately to wrest that dominion away from him. Sometimes this is expressed quite forcefully.

God called the Hebrew Prophet Isaiah to preach to his people. He urges him to make the heart of the people fat, their ears heavy, and to shut their eyes, lest they use these faculties to turn again in obedience and so be healed (Isaiah 6:9–10). This looks strongly like fatalism, but is surely bitter irony. Why send Isaiah to prophesy if people would not hear and be transformed?

Centuries later, Jesus quoted this passage in a parable about the reception of his own teaching (Mark 4:12). He admitted ruefully that though some would hear and follow his words successfully, many more would not. Again, the context indicates irony, not predestination. Later interpretations of Christianity sometimes stressed fatalism, not least certain branches of Calvinism, movements often loosely based on the teaching of the Protestant reformer John Calvin (1509–64).

Much of the language of the Quran seems fatalistic. 9:51 records that nothing will befall a person except what God has written. Yet 18:23 urges hearers not to say what they are going to do tomorrow except for the rider 'If God wills'. That expression, in Arabic *In Shaa Allah*, is often used by Muslims. Outsiders often see it as fatalistic in intention. Yet it need not be; nor need the Quranic verse be, from which it comes. Rather, Muslims recognise that their response is within boundaries set by God. Those boundaries include the creation and sustaining of the world, the sense that life and death are more within the gift of God than the desire of individual humans.

There are many things a person can choose to do, but there are many things she cannot. Indeed, it might be argued that some customs of religious law or tradition, those (for example) which prescribe who you can marry or what you can eat, are a reminder that even matters over which one has a theoretical control ought to be ceded to the will of God who gives life and deals death. Later Muslim theologians stressed the will of God to the point where human responsibility seemed unimportant. For example, the doctrine of *kasb* (acquisition) was a brave effort by medieval theologians to reconcile, on the one hand, God's control over events with, on the other, human free will and responsibility for one's own actions. According to this doctrine, God creates actions but humans 'acquire' them.

In fact, most religions imply where they do not affirm some element of human choice. Many Jewish teachers have commented that, if people cannot freely choose, how can they be commanded in the Torah to do good and not evil? Even so, medieval Jewish philosophers struggled, as did their Christian and Muslim counterparts, with the problem of reconciling God's foreknowledge with human free will.

To some extent, this is a language game. Language is a human construct conveying as best it can the mysteries of Transcendence. Philosophers and theologians often try to use words in relatively precise ways. Prophets and scriptures deal in humour, irony, exaggeration, and other means of evoking from their audience a sense of the ultimate. So it is not surprising that they often seem to be contradictory. Their aim is not consistency but transformation. Sometimes, apparent inconsistencies co-exist side by side. The Quran 13:27 runs: 'Unbelievers say, "Why isn't a sign sent down to him from his Lord?" Say: "In truth God leaves to wander whom he wills; but guides to himself those who turn in contrition." ' This paradox could be illustrated by material from Christianity, Judaism, and most of the world's religions.

As we noted in chapter 1, John Bowker has asked searching questions about religions as the earliest form of gene-replicating and nurturing cultural systems. Genetic research has transferred to the scientific arena a question long asked by the world's religions about the extent to which humans are free agents. There is no necessary reason why religion and science should be antagonistic towards each other; only a recent Western history that has made them so. Indeed, in medieval times scientific enquiry flourished under Muslim rule. It may be that religion and science could together reflect upon this issue of free will and fatalism. Common sense suggests that all humans lead circumscribed lives. For instance, I am white, male, middle-class, and English. Of those adjectives, only 'middle-class' defines a status over which I have any control, and even then, only a very little. Yet, within those constraints, I can make significant choices about how to construct, commit and live my life. Other people, of course, have much less choice possible to them. The poor and, in many societies, women, live lives that are quite other than they might pick. Yet for most, admittedly not all, people, there is some choice open to them. At their best, religions negotiate a course between affirming complete human freedom and the utter power of Transcendent will by affirming that, within the constraints upon humans, there is room for obedience and spiritual growth.

Transcendence is not always best understood by those of a literal cast of mind, who have no sense of the disciplined imagination or any intuitive skills. Such devotees are often profoundly destructive of others. We shall see this in our discussion about fundamentalism in the next and final chapter.

a universal rule?

Is there a common ethic underlying all religious endeavour and experience? This question has become increasingly urgent in a world under the threat of nuclear annihilation. If humans could point to a common thread of teaching that seems to be how Transcendence lures humans towards the good, then we might be able to promote the things that make for peace. Some have located this in the Golden or Universal Rule. This is the teaching that we should treat others as we ourselves would wish to be treated. So the Native American Great Law of Peace runs 'The foundation is respect for all life'; and the Analects of Confucius (15:23) asserts that 'Do not unto others what you would not have them do unto you'. This can be paralleled in most or maybe even all religious traditions. (The variant forms of this universal rule are set out especially well in Fisher, 1999; p.104.)

There are two reservations to be made. The first is that, as we have already recognised, religions do not always practise what they preach. In the concluding chapter, we shall note rising fundamentalism in the world's religions. Advocates of this phenomenon are not over-scrupulous about their treatment of those who disagree with them. And any survey of the history of religions would note, not only human lives transformed for the better, but also human lives destroyed in the name of religion.

Secondly, there is a tendency among the proponents of the Golden Rule to offer easy, over-simplistic ways through complex ethical, political and social relations between the religions. Distinguished enthusiasts like Hans Küng and Leonard Swidler have located the Golden Rule in many religions, and proffer it as a cure for the world's ills. They designate it as the foundation for a Global Ethic. I am not so sure. The first-century BCE Rabbi Hillel must have been a wonderfully quirky man. For example, some people tried to irritate him by asking him silly questions. One said: 'Why do Babylonians have round heads?' 'My son, you have asked a great question,' he replied, 'because they have no skilful midwives.' He used humour as part of his teaching method to defuse animosity and to get others to think and move beyond their trite assumptions: he was, after all, Jewish, and Jewish humour is renowned. When a heathen came to him to ask him to teach him the whole Torah standing on one leg, Hillel replied: 'That which is hateful to you do not do to your neighbour. This is the whole of the Torah. The rest is commentary.' Serious-minded proponents of a Global Ethic have pounced on this as the Jewish illustration of a universal impulse towards a Golden Rule. Yet I speculate that Hillel accepted the essentially trivial approach of this seeker after truth in palatable form, so as, by wit and wisdom, to lead him deeper into the ocean of truth.

So if humans genuinely seek peace in the world, it is important not to be sentimental and simplistic about core values, and foolish to locate agreement and even difference between religions in the wrong places. For certain, we need not only an ethic of agreement but also an ethic for coping with disagreement, where religions have wronged others. For example, Dalits in India, the oppressed or burdened ones, marginalised and even dehumanised by many other Indians, have little reason to value or trust the teachings of the Sanskritic traditions of Hinduism. The Nazi Holocaust that killed six million Jews between 1942 and 1945 was justified by the centuries-old Christian teaching of contempt against Jews. Any ethic we pursue that would ensure the world's survival has to recognise the need for justice towards other humans and also the integrity of creation, and avoid any spurious harmonisation that papers over profound inequities.

A lot of sentimental and unfocused writing has emerged in the last few years on the topic of a Global Ethic. Some works (e.g. Twiss and Grelle, 1998, *passim*) are beginning to address in a tough minded way some of the hard issues that the possibility of a Global Ethic raises: is it the pursuit of the comfortably off, diverting them from really helping the poor? Is it Western, post-Christian and secular? Does it neuter the religious ethics of a particular tradition for an ineffective common core? Have religious people really understood that certain forms of religion are part of the problem of the world's ills more than convincing cures? It is also important to address particular issues that are of concern in our day and age. They include: human rights; the role of women; the environment; international business; the gulf between science and religion; and so on.

The Global Ethic is a brave and admirable attempt to harness the resources of the world's religions to positive and universal ends. Yet religions cannot just be applied like balm for the soul in order to produce desirable ends like peace and justice. They must not simply admire their theoretical resources. They have to reform themselves in the contemporary world, if they are truly to be homes for the human spirit. They must learn from each other, and explore each other's deepest resources for faithful adaptation to the context of our global village. It may well be that the way of the mystics or a study of cross-cultural spiritualities or even the Perennial Philosophy may provide a more enduring foundation for a Global Ethic than the Golden Rule.

what sort of god is god?

The question is theistically put. We could ask it in a more cumbersome but inclusive way. Something like this perhaps: given that fact that most humans argue about Transcendence, whether it is personal or impersonal, wholly other or the great stream of being in which we are all droplets, can we nevertheless infer anything about Transcendent reality from what it requires of us?

The most obvious inference is that Transcendence sets a limited diversity open to us. All humans are located in a time and place, constrained by social, economic and other (including religious!) factors. Yet we have a choice: to work with Transcendence or to ignore or even disobey its alluring summons. Clearly, the choices open to an Indian peasant working in an urban slum to keep herself and her family alive are different than that of her near neighbour who has a university degree and a secure, well-paid job. Yet happiness, faithfulness, goodness and commitment can flourish in unexpected places, among the poor as well as the wealthy. Impressive religious figures can teach us this in a very matter-of-fact, unsentimental way. Prince Siddharth gave up excessive wealth, but also saw through the puerile claims of those who lauded excessive poverty or asceticism, to become the Buddha, a wandering teacher of enlightenment. Jesus of Nazareth ignored the nearby, prosperous conurbation of Sepphoris and taught the peasants of Galilee. He told one rich young man that his wealth was an encumbrance to him, but did not utterly condemn riches. Even today a holy man like Baba Virsa Singh, who has a farm outside Delhi, meets rich and poor alike, who come for his wit, wisdom and blessing. So it would seem that Transcendence seeks all sorts and conditions of people.

Transcendence captivates, allures, persuades people to her worship and service. That service usually has a strong ethical component. Those who respond to her by seeking to live the good life, so religions variously affirm, find perfect freedom, know her, find their highest obedience in her, are set free by the truth, show kindness, give to a neighbourhood its beauty. The sort of Transcendence they intuit her to be makes them the sort of people they can become by her alluring grace and power.

religion in the new millennium

Thirteen hundred years before the Common Era, the Pharaoh Akhenaten ruled Egypt. We have seen that he changed the religion of his ancestors and worshipped the disc of the sun as the symbol of the one God, Aten. He was possibly the first ever important believer in one God, rather than many gods.

Akhenaten died without an obvious male heir, and his religion died with him. It has been the fate of most religions to flourish and then die. Some survive for centuries, a few for a thousand years or longer. But most if not all sink into the sands of time, just as the relics of Akhenaten's faith were buried beneath the sands of Egypt's desert, only to be resurrected today as museum pieces in Luxor and a few other places.

No religion has the privilege to survive forever, even if its members think they are right and everyone else is wrong. The religion of Ancient Egypt survived Akhenaten's 'experiment'. Indeed, it lasted longer than any other human way of faith, from its origins at the beginning of the third millennium BCE to about the fourth century CE. Other great religions flourish and fade, sometimes to the point of extinction, though often aspects are appropriated into new religious forms. Although contemporary Christianity flourishes in parts of Africa and Asia, in its ancient heartland of Europe and West Asia it is often in a sorry state of decline. Similarly, Islam is in the ascendancy in large parts of the world, but it too has known times of decay and decline and will doubtless do so again. The great world faiths of today, not just Christianity and Islam, but Judaism, Buddhism, Hinduism and others, have waxed and waned. One day, they may fade away, as did the religion of Akhenaten, and his enemies, and the religion of the Aztecs, the Incas, the ancient Greeks and many more.

Sometimes, we think that because our religion survives, it must be better than ones that have died. But many Roman soldiers at the time of Jesus must have thought that their belief in Mithras, a god popular in the Roman Empire, was better than that of the Greeks, the Jews and the Christians, because, under Mithras, Rome had flourished. Now Mithraism has long sunk into the dust. To paraphrase a passage from the Quran: all things pass away (certainly, human beings; even long-standing religions), save for the face of God.

A few years ago, in Christianity, there was a movement that proclaimed 'God is dead'. Predictably, God still lives in the heart of believers, but that movement is dead. Again, this goes to show that it is not God who dies, but religions. What should that tell us at the start of a new millennium? The most obvious thing, yet the hardest for any human to apprehend and heed, is that all religions are human constructs. Stating this distinct fact does not affirm the views of those secularists who believe that religions convey nothing of importance, but represent only the flickering fears of humans who are unable to come to terms with their own mortality. We have already seen reasons to undermine this theory: if Karl Marx and Sigmund Freud had had a deeper understanding of their own religion, they could not have popularised some of their more shallow views about the origin of religion. A recognition that religions are human constructs takes seriously the fact that it is through the works of human hands, hearts and imaginations that Transcendence makes her presence felt. If people are to implement a religious vision for humankind, indeed for all creation, it is a joint enterprise between them and God or Brahman or however Transcendence is named. There are two errors religious (and other) humans make about religion. The first is that it is entirely the work of Transcendence, to which humans can only respond in wonder, love and praise. At worst, this has led people into defending their prejudice and their culture, but also, alas, their highest and noblest aspirations and attainments as if they exhausted the ways by which Transcendence engages with all it has created. At their best, people of faith have recognised that there is more than meets their eye, not only to life, but even to what their religion reveals of that 'more'. The other extreme error is that religions are only poetry and myth, at best encouraging noble deeds, creative thought and even (to some extent) transformed imaginations. Somewhere between these positions lies the view that humankind's artefacts of religions are porous to the presence of divine grace and will, to those who are attuned to his alluring presence.

How are contemporary humans to find religion to be a transformative experience? Well, let us begin by briefly exploring the world we live in today, which in significant ways is quite different from the world of even the relatively recent past. Our world is in a rapid process of globalisation. Since the end of the Second World War, enormous changes have been taking place, which seem to increase exponentially. European colonial rule over much of the world has largely ended. The creation of new nation-states has led not only to burgeoning nationalism, but also a growth in self-confidence among many religions. New Diasporas have led to the establishment of members of many religions in new places, where they are rooting themselves in a variety of cultures alien to their places of origin. The growth of information technology and the increasing ease of transport by car and plane for many people have also made the world seem smaller and more interconnected.

Much change has been positive. Much has not. Western economic imperialism seems to have replaced its political predecessor over much of the globe. Some people live in luxury in London, New York, Beijing, Mumbai and elsewhere, but can look out and see beggars close by. Social, economic and political inequities seem as great as ever, if not more so. How, then, is religion responding to the transformed and transforming world of today, on the cusp of the third millennium?

When discussing, in chapter 4, the hope of some people in the creation of a Global Ethic, I noted issues that remain for religions to deal with in the contemporary world. They include: human rights; the role of women; the environment; international business; the gulf between science and religion; and so on. These matters cannot be dealt with only by individual religions. Indeed, the aspiration towards a Global Ethic illustrates the implicit or explicit conviction in some religious people that religions must work together if the world is to flourish or even just survive. Though these are important issues, they will be dealt with in my book, *Inter-religious Dialogue: A Short Introduction*, which examines the need for dialogue in the contemporary world, to overcome issues of injustice and bigotry.

In this chapter, I propose to look at trends in contemporary religion, under the subtitles 'Idealisation of the Past' and 'Diasporas', 'Reconstructions of Religion' and 'The Search for Justice'. Then we shall look at the question of truth and the importance of faith.

idealisation of the past

A common response of religious people to the enormous changes afoot in the contemporary world is to retreat into the past. This can be seen in the rise of religious fundamentalism. Fundamentalism is rather a slippery word. It was originally used about the reactionary responses of certain North American Christians to the opinions of more liberal Christians, in the early years of the twentieth century. It has since been used, often rather indiscriminately, of members of many faiths whose views are less 'progressive' than their 'opponents' would wish. Most religious people would have no qualms about being called fundamentalists, in the sense that they follow the fundamentals of their faith.

The point at issue is what is fundamental to a religion. Fundamentalists look for inerrancy: the certain word of truth from God; the vision of how things ultimately are that brooks no refusal and offers no alternative. Such certainty deals in simplicity. It is certainly true, for example, that Orthodox Jews hold that the Pentateuch is God's word, and that the vast majority of Muslims hold the Quran to be so. Yet such Jews and Muslims have often interpreted how it is so with great subtlety. Jews regard Mishnah and Talmud as containing illustrations of how it has been interpreted. Muslims have developed *tafsir* literature, which comments upon the meaning and relevance of the sacred text. Indeed, many Muslims hold that the hadith literature, traditions of what the Prophet Muhammad said and did, according to his earliest followers, is a second holy writ, which contextualises and explicates the meaning of the Quran. Such traditionalists are to be differentiated from fundamentalists, who believe that their point of view, often simplistic, always culturally conditioned and easy for them to understand, is better than the accumulated wisdom of tradition or any form of open-mindedness. So they ride roughshod over that tradition, either by asserting that faithful people should go back to basics and ignore centuries of (in their opinion) misinterpretation, or else they declare that tradition is uniform and speaks only one opinion and with one voice. This is simply not true. The Talmud, for example, contains many divergent voices, as does *tafsir* literature, and the Christian Bible. Indeed, the stated or implied conviction of many mainstream believers is that the interpretative process in which many voices engage with tradition does not destroy truth but allows it to emerge.

The twentieth century has been an era of extraordinary political, social and economic change. Fundamentalism can be seen as a rather frightened response to such change. Yet no more than King Canute, seated by the seashore, could force the waves to go back when his officials told him he could, can frightened people find real security in religious simplicities. Such a reductionist faith often ignores what many see as the heart of religion. There is, for example, not a great deal of love among Christians who are fundamentalist for those who hold other views. This is true, even though the word *agape* was interpreted in the New Testament to mean a love for others based upon God's love for his creation, an extension of that word's original meaning. Also, there is not much trust in the will of God to accomplish what he will, by those Muslims who feel impelled to enforce a particular and narrow view of it in shrill and violent ways.

This idealisation and simplifying of the religious past can affect liberals as well as conservatives. The convictions of some Christians that, for example, the heart of religion is Jesus' Sermon on the Mount, or that Paul distorted the essentially simple message of Jesus, are cases in point. Moreover, liberals, ironically, can be illiberal when it comes to defending their views against other ones. The reaction to Muslims and to the faith of Islam by some secularised writers when the Ayatollah Khomeini issued a *fatwa* against Salman Rushdie in 1989, illustrated their ignorance and intolerance of 'otherness'. To admit this does not, of course, condone the action of the Ayatollah or those who unheedingly supported him.

Perhaps we can distinguish liberals from fundamentalists in this way. Secularised liberals base their simplicities on a premise that human beings ought essentially to be endlessly open and accommodating towards others, and often believe that religion is a hindrance to this desirable outcome. Religious liberals emphasise the tolerant and open-minded aspects of their religion, sometimes at the expense of other of its teachings. Fundamentalists often seem to need an enemy: either others of their faith who do not share their position, or those outsiders.

Each religion is a more subtle and diverse phenomenon than many secularists and even many religious people believe. Religions are at their best when they recognise human limitations at grasping truth, and, as the Christian Apostle Paul put it, affirm that 'my knowledge now is partial; then it will be whole, like God's knowledge of me' (1 Cor. 13:12). Religious people should accept mystery in religion, not seek a simplified mastery of it. It may be that even some though by no means all of the proponents of the Perennial Philosophy and of mysticism too easily fall into the trap of idealising the past.

Many practitioners of the New Age Movement also deal with the past in a simplified and romanticised way. This movement grew up in the West in the 1960s, though its roots lie further back in the past. Indeed, because many of its practitioners use religious symbolism from ancient India and Egypt, they regard it as an old religion. It is very much a pluriform religious phenomenon. Its practitioners may resort to: channelling the powers of a dead figure to speak to the living; the use of crystals and other artefacts to uncover a person's desires; alternative medicine; Shamanism, Paganism and Zen Buddhism. To many new-agers, ecological issues and the feminine are important. They often see Christianity as a foe. It belongs to the age of Pisces (for astrology is usually an important New-Age phenomenon), to be replaced by the age of Aquarius.

Many members of the 'Old-Age' religions view New Ageism with scepticism. It seems to them like religion on the cheap. You take a dash of religion from Egypt, stir it with an insight from India, add a touch of wisdom from Japan and China, throw in Native American Sweat-Lodge ceremonies, and thereby hope to produce authentic religion. Whilst these things are convincing and authoritative in the context in which they emerge, as filtered through New Age aspirations, they can look like the hobby of white, middle-class dilettantes with too much time and money, and not enough real commitment.

Nevertheless, the phenomenon indicates that, if mainstream religion cannot easily meet the aspirations of many relatively affluent Westerners, austere forms of secularism that would totally exclude the Transcendent are just as deficient in their eyes. Time will tell whether parts of the New Age Movement will contribute to reconstructions of religion that will cause religion to survive and flourish in the new millennium, or whether it is a transient phenomenon.

reconstructions of religion

Other reconstructions of religion are more focused and less 'pick and mix' than the opportunities offered by the New Age Movement. Many first peoples of the world look to the roots of their faith to sustain them. Common to the many and various forms of such themes is a strong conviction of humans as an integral part of creation. Thus they retain a respect for nature through living a sustainable and co-operative way of life. In many parts of the world, they seek to prevent governments and firms from polluting the land by plundering natural resources or by financing and encouraging a heavy growth in tourism and its attendant industries.

In North America, a number of people of mixed race, part Native American and maybe part White, identify more with their first peoples' heritage than with secularism or Christian faith. This can look like an idealisation of the past, and in some cases it likely is. But it need not be. With the growth of global warming, environmental pollution, and other related problems, such a choice seems like dealing with realities of the present. Many such believers affirm that only an appropriate spirituality can overcome many powerful humans' proud and misplaced trust in technology to solve all the problems of the world. In their view, scientific problem solving cannot by itself mend the wounds of the world. Indeed, Pacific islanders, for example, have reason to know that their environment can be threatened by the arrogant use of their surroundings for nuclear testing by a far-away Western government.

Many first people are deeply suspicious of Christianity as a religion. Christians by conviction or heritage plundered their land, annihilated many of their forebears, and dispossessed them of their material and spiritual heritage. They view Christianity as too obsessed by a will for human domination of creation rather than by seeking to live in harmony and partnership with other species and with mother-Earth herself. (See the article by Walking Bear Woman, also known as Voyce Durling Jones, in Forward, 1995, pp.81–91.)

Many religions locate a reverence for creation at their heart. Indeed, although Judaism, Christianity and Islam interpret humans as rulers of creation on God's behalf, at their best they encourage and sustain humans to act as part of all things with the creator's grace and care. One strand of Hinduism interprets the universe as part of the body of God, so that all things are suffused with and sustained by Transcendent power and deserve respect and care.

Another form of reconstruction of religion can be found in South Asia. The last century has seen a number of neo-Hindu and other movements that have attempted to bring that religion and others up to date for contemporary needs. One such need is to universalise their message. Many South Asian forms of religion are rooted to the soil of India, so that, until relatively recently, many traditionalists believed it was impossible to translate them wider afield. This was the case, even though Hindus were present in considerable numbers in other parts of Asia, and in South Africa. When the great Mahatma Gandhi returned from England to India in 1891, he underwent ritual purification to shed the pollution of foreign travel. Nowadays, there are many ways of South Asian faith that have much wider appeal.

One example is from Sikhism. When I made radio programmes for the BBC World Service, I went to Gobind Sadan, a farm just outside Delhi. My friend, Mary Pat Fisher, introduced me to Gobind Sadan. She is an American, whose earliest experiences of religious commitment had been in a Methodist Church. That outer form of religion provided her with no inner connection to God, which then she found in nature not faith. Over twenty years ago, she survived a close encounter with death. In her hospital room, she discovered a great Presence, Light and Power, unconditional Love, to whom she offered the rest of her life. She became the publisher of a small book company producing spiritual works. Indeed, she wrote a widely-used and influential textbook called *Living Religions,* based on her encounters with Christianity, Buddhism, Sufism, Judaism, Taoism, Hinduism and nature religions.

Then came the most fateful day of her life, 23 July 1990. She was invited to interview Baba Virsa Singh for her global radio programme 'Earthcare'. She was very impressed by him, and accepted his invitation to an interfaith seminar on meditation, held at Gobind Sadan. There, the evident love on people's faces and their devotion to God and to Baba Virsa Singh captivated her. Gobind Sadan is one a number of farms that Baba Virsa Singh has reclaimed from barren lands with the aid of his own intuitive wisdom, and the hard work of his followers. No outside money is ever taken. People who come are welcome at the communal kitchen. I am one of many who has been put up for a few nights at no charge, and fed a simple sustaining vegetarian diet.

Baba Virsa Singh is known affectionately as Babaji ('respected father') or Maharaj ji ('King of kings'). In this life (for he believes that he, like us all, lives many), he is illiterate, a Punjabi farmer. He was born a Sikh, and Sikh spirituality colours his daily life and the devotions of his followers. Many recite the Jaap Sahib, a prayer of the tenth Sikh guru, seven times a day; each recitation takes about twenty minutes. At Gobind Sadan, devotions take place several times a day, beginning at 2am.

Mary Pat identifies him as the living embodiment of the love, truth and power at the heart of the universe, which she had first encountered many years before, on her sickbed in hospital. Although he is a Sikh, Babaji points out to others the eternal verities embedded in their own traditions. Referring to his, the Sikh scripture, he comments: 'When we fully understand Guru Granth Sahib, the walls of hatred will fall down at once, because God is not contained within any one religion.' Indeed, Babaji insists that all religions are human constructs. What is best in each of them points to and reveals God.

Many religious leaders of other faiths come to listen to and speak with Babaji. They include: Syed Ausuf Ali, a Muslim Sufi scholar who taught at Hamdard University; the late Paulos Mar Gregorios, Metropolitan of Delhi and the North in the Malankara Orthodox Church and a former President of the World Council of Churches; Dr Karan Singh, a distinguished Hindu and the last princely ruler of the State of Jammu and Kashmir; and many more. These are not simple, credulous people. They are eminent intellectuals and religious leaders yet, when I talked with them, each saw in Babaji a saint and a sage, one of those people who, throughout India's long

Baba Virsa Singh

religious history, bring people together through their extraordinary powers, including the persuasive and captivating force of love.

Politicians come to see him too. In an interview, the late Surendra Nath, then Governor of the Punjab, revealed how often he came to consult Babaji about his difficult job, controlling a state then riven by faction and violence. He had long sought a guru, and when he met Baba Virsa Singh, it was love at first sight; he knew he had come home. This eminent politician and public servant found time to translate the Jaap Sahib into English. He saw his guru as someone who can look into the past, present and the future. He testified to the number of people whom he knew had been cured of fatal illnesses by Babaji. Yet he maintained that the greatest miracle was the transformation of people into better human beings.

One of Babaji's earliest followers was Swaranjit Singh, an engineer and businessman. He explained how Babaji had chosen Gobind Sadan in 1969. This was a rocky and barren area, which everyone said was no good for farming. Yet Babaji located a spot and told people to dig, where they found water. With the aid of only three tractors, people laboured eighteen hours a day to turn it into fertile soil.

When Babaji is at Gobind Sadan, he holds a daily audience with people by a waterfall which he has had built. There he gives instruction to enquirers after truth. I met him there on one occasion. I talked afterwards with a doctor and two dentists, as well as many non-professional people, some of whom had travelled long distances to see him. Later, I went to pray and meditate at Jesus' place, an area within Gobind Sadan where Jesus appeared to Babaji. On my way there, Baba Virsa Singh passed me with some other people. He turned and gave a smile of immense radiance, sweetness and charm. He often interprets words of the great religious leaders of humankind, including Jesus. One of his renditions is of a man who, impressed by Jesus' nature miracles, asked him who he was. Jesus replied, 'I am nothing. The difference between you and me is that I have faith. You think that you are doing things, but I know that everything is under my Father's command.'

The permanent residents of Gobind Sadan are about forty people, rich and poor, educated and illiterate, who share simple rooms and eat from a common kitchen. Their work, which is supported by income from large farms elsewhere, enables Babaji to exercise his ministry among the many people who stream to this place to meet and hear him. These visitors now include several Prime Ministers, great politicians and other religious people. They also number illiterate people, labourers, artisans and professional people; human beings from all walks of life. All come expectantly, yearning for religious insight and revelation. Most seem to believe that they have received it.

It is difficult to tell whether some Asian transformations of religion, such as that expounded by Baba Virsa Singh, qualify as New Religious Movements, or as interpretations of an ancient religion. To some extent, it depends on the hospitality of the 'home' religion. Because Asian religions are often more 'open-ended' and tolerant of luxurious, internal growth than Semitic religions, movements like Babaji's are often (though by no means always) more acceptable to the religious majority than happens in Judaism, Christianity and Islam. For example, the movements of the 1840s in European Jewry began the process of creating Orthodoxy and other forms out of the Judaism of previous centuries. Still today, there is much disagreement between different forms of (often self-designated) Orthodox Jews about the status of other Jews as Jews.

Mainstream religions have in fact undergone enormous transformations and reconstructions in the modern world. Perhaps the best example is the Roman Catholic Church. Pope John XXIII, whose pontificate was from 1958 to 1965, began the reforms of the Second Vatican Council, which concluded in 1965. Among widespread reforms were: improved relations with other Christian denominations and with other religions; the replacement of the vernacular for Latin in the Mass; and the introduction (and occasionally the implementation) of the principle of collegiality in church government.

diasporas

One present reality within contemporary religion is a growth in religious Diasporas. This is not a new phenomenon. In the past, Jews have scattered over large parts of the globe; Hindus have spread into Eastern Asia; Buddhists, Christians and Muslims have become indigenous in many societies. Yet, in our global village, where people now move much more freely for economic and other reasons (sometimes as refugees), new questions are being asked about how to be faithful as, for example, a Muslim of South Asian origin in Orange County, California; or a Hindu in Leicester.

A Jewish scholar has recently argued that Judaism's great gift to the world may be Diaspora rather than monotheism (Boyarin, 1994; p.258). This is an intriguing thought. Yet for contemporary Jews, there is a certain irony in the fact that the creation of the State of Israel in 1948 has led to the uprooting of long-standing Jewish communities elsewhere, since many have left the lands of their birth and gone to Israel to put down roots there. This process of uprooting began, appallingly, in the Holocaust. When the Second World War ended in 1945, so had a whole way of life for European Jews. Their numbers were decimated. Of the prewar Jewish populations of Poland, Latvia, Lithuania, Estonia, Germany and Austria, less than ten per cent survived; and less than thirty per cent of Jews in occupied Russia, Ukraine, Belgium, Yugoslavia, Norway and Rumania.

One particularly poignant example of Jewish depopulation in the years since 1945 has been that of Indian Jews. The oldest synagogue in the Commonwealth is in Cochin, a town in the South Indian State of Kerala. The building is in an area called Jewtown, a name that might have racist connotations in Europe but is happily accepted by the Jews who live there. Its narrow streets and shops do in fact remind one of Jewish areas in certain European cities. The synagogue has some unusual features. It has two pulpits, a feature unique to the synagogues of Kerala, twelve windows for the twelve tribes of Israel, and two pillars named after the two pillars of the first temple in Jerusalem, destroyed by Babylonian invaders in 587 BCE.

Nobody really knows who were the first Jews to arrive in India. It is possible that they were a group called the Bene Israel. There was active trading two thousand years ago between Israel and India. The story goes that a group of seven men and seven women was shipwrecked on the coast of Maharashtra, in north-western India. The group settled there and later generations continued to observe Jewish rites, though members borrowed local Hindu customs and intermarried with Hindus and Muslims.

Alternatively, the Cochin Jews, descendants of a group that landed at the ancient port of Cranganore, maintain that they were the first Jews to settle in India. Some claim that the Cranganore Jews arrived on King Solomon's merchant fleet, almost three thousand years ago. Others suggest that Jews fled there after the destruction of the first Temple. Moses de Paiva, a Dutch Jew who visited Cochin on 21 November 1686, wrote that 70,000 to 80,000 Jews had arrived in the area in 378 CE from Majorca, where their ancestors had been taken after the destruction of the second Temple in 70 CE. Ten thousand of them were graciously received by the local Hindu ruler and allowed to settle throughout the area, though most made their homes in Cranganore. There are some copper plates kept in the Cochin synagogue whose actual age is disputed but they are old enough to show that the Jewish community has been present for many centuries. The plates, written in an ancient language, granted rights to a Jewish leader to have his own palanquin and drums, a privilege that was usually given to minor rulers.

Wherever they settled, the Jews found South Asia to be a place of refuge from persecution. Many of their ancestors had fled there from the Christian inquisition in Spain. Like many Spanish Jews, they came late in the sixteenth century, through Aleppo in Syria. The Portuguese landed in Kerala in 1600 and an early zealot wrote to the King of Portugal informing him of the large number of Jews there and asking his permission to exterminate them one by one as he came across them. Fortunately, that request came to nothing. Another wave of Jewish settlers came to India at the end of the eighteenth century. Their descendants call themselves Baghdadi Jews. They arrived in Bombay from Iraq in the wake of persecution by Ottoman Turkish rulers. The Jewish ruler there, the Exilarch, was persecuted and, as a result, Sheikh Sassoon and his son David left Baghdad. After his father died, David, hearing of the benevolence of the British and the freedom of trade they gave to areas in their control, came to India. He became known as the Merchant Prince of India. He was in need of personnel to work in his mills and factories, so he imported Jews to the Bombay area.

I went to South Asia in 1992, to make radio programmes for the BBC World Service on minority religions in the subcontinent. One common note struck by all the Jews I interviewed was gratitude to British tolerance but even more to Hindu open-mindedness and magnanimity. One woman told me that there was no question of Jews living in ghettos. Hindus, she averred, are the most tolerant of people. Another Jew in Cochin told me that the Kerala Jews have been a pampered people. They were given preferential treatment in education and, as a result, have always considered themselves as Indian. An elderly Jewish woman who lives in Bombay, summed it up thus: 'I can honestly say that India is the only country that I am aware of where we Jews have never experienced the bitterness of anti-Semitism.'

The sense of a glorious past echoes through the words of South Asian Jews, but their numbers are now in steep decline. When the State of Israel was founded in 1948, it offered Jewish nationality to any Jew who settled there. Seized by the vision of a new homeland, many Orthodox Jews from Kerala and Bombay emigrated there. India itself had gained independence from British rule just a year before and some Indian Jews felt that Israel needed them more than the land of their birth. In the wake of widespread emigration to Israel, other young South Asian Jews went to Canada, the USA, Great Britain and other countries.

A great sense of nostalgia pervades older Jews in South Asia. That elderly Jewish woman in Bombay reminisced about the thriving Jewish community in the Bombay of her youth. But it dwindled away, so that when she went to her son's wedding in Israel in 1982, the contrast between Jews there and at home struck her forcibly. She said that the last Jewish wedding in Bombay had been two years before, and was between a widower of sixty-five and a woman of a similar age. There are now no young Jews in Bombay. She remembered that in the 1940s there were about 15,000 Jews in India, but now the Babylonian Jews find it difficult to make up a *minyan* – the ten men necessary for a religious service. To perform this and other religious duties they have to call on the help of the Bene Israel; rather reluctantly, since they regard them as unorthodox. The Jewish community seems to contemplate its own imminent demise in Bombay with a certain stoicism. In Kerala too there has been a spectacular decline in the number of Jews. In the 1940s there were about 2500 Jews in eight congregations. Now there are only a few Jews left.

Of all the communities I researched, interviewed, and made programmes about, the Jews of South Asia formed the most poignant. That same Bombay woman was, in her own old age, learning to make shrouds for the few remaining members of her community so that they could be properly buried. Who would make hers, she wondered? The Jews of India were fascinating to me because they face their fate bleakly out of a hopeful history.

How painfully incongruous it is that the days of Jewish settlement in South Asia seem to be numbered. There is a certain irony in the fact that Jews may disappear from the one land that has always welcomed them; not because of the government's policy but because of the Jews' own actions in response to the creation of the State of Israel.

the search for justice

Israel has become a beacon of hope to many Jews in the wake of the Holocaust. It seems to guarantee safety, and a place where they can live in justice and peace. Ironically, this is not how Palestinian Muslims and Christians see it, many of whom feel victimised and even colonised. The history of Israel since 1948 has been a continuing search for justice and peace, within the context of the question: who are these virtues for? Only a section or the whole of society?

Liberation and feminist theologies in Christianity have had an effect on other faiths: to some extent, on Jewish, Muslim and Buddhist thinkers. Liberation theology began about thirty years ago in South America, blending Christian theology and Marxism to improve the social, economic and political situation of the poor and dispossessed. It has spread widely.

One of its most interesting and thought-provoking forms is in India. There, Dalits, the 'pressed down', are the so-called 'scheduled castes'. The Hindu caste system locates them as outcastes, below the fourfold overarching structure of Brahmin priests, Kshatriya ruler-warriors, Vaishya merchants and farmers, and Shudra servants. They form about twenty per cent of India's population, maybe two hundred million souls. They have been called 'untouchables', whose touch or even shadow pollutes caste Hindus; therefore, they have been banned from many wells, villages and temples and have been assigned the most menial occupations.

It is fascinating to reflect that, whereas Jews have found Hindus to be the most hospitable and tolerant of neighbours, others have not. It is not just the 'outcaste' who has suffered in this respect. Upon independence from Britain, India became a secular state; not secular in the sense of anti-religious, but in the sense of providing a boundary within which all people, of any religion or none, can flourish. In recent reaction to this, some Hindus have drawn upon more exclusive and intolerant interpretations of Indian faith. Political and religious groups have sought, and to some extent obtained, a more Hindu focus in national life. This is quite understandable, given that the overwhelming number of Indians are Hindus. Difficulties arise, however, when the assertion of *hindutva*, Hindu identity, entails the marginalisation or even persecution and killing of others, be they Muslim, Christian or of other faiths. More chilling illustrations can be found in the Balkans and Sri Lanka and many parts of the world, where the resurgence of religion does not seem to lead to justice for all, but only the promotion of the beliefs and rights of the more powerful group or groups.

In India, the growth of Dalit theology has expressed the hope for justice for the oppressed. Over the last few years, I have made a couple of radio programmes on the Dalits, and will refer to material I collected for them throughout the rest of this section. Although the Dalits span many religions, because the caste system has affected many more religions than Hinduism, it is Dalit Christians who have worked most to ameliorate their own plight. When I interviewed him for a radio programme, the Church of South India Bishop Azariah of Madras was a silver-tongued orator. He graphically described how Dalits labour under the caste system. He saw it as a pyramid, with a base provided by the Dalits, who have no staircase to the top. So others crush them. He maintained that of the thirty million Christians in India, sixty-five per cent are Dalits. The Hindu notion of *karma*, the belief that people's past lives continue to influence the present life, has often been used to justify the conviction that Dalits deserve the poverty and degradation in which they live. Yet, in his view, what *karma* cannot change, God can.

Yet God has to work against two millennia of transmitted prejudice. So what can be done to improve the social and economic lot of Dalits? Henry Thiagaraj, Director of the Dalit Liberation Education Trust based in Madras, told me that there is abundant evidence of the Dalits having a wounded psyche; with oppression comes depression. Many are depressed to the extent that they will not help themselves. They believe nothing has ever changed to improve their lot, and nothing ever will. He works to change that attitude, particularly among young people. He took me to a rural area, where there was a work camp for young Dalits in their teens and twenties. It was a remarkable and moving experience to see them talking together, laughing and dancing. One young man told me that he now had the confidence to believe in the future, because he had made friends with whom he could work to change the social, economic and religious oppression of centuries.

Because this religious oppression focuses upon the caste system, many Dalits particularly abhor Hinduism. Bishop Azariah bluntly affirmed that the Dalits have a more spiritual religion than the Hindus do. Henry Thiagaraj described this Dalit spirituality. It has little to do with the Sanskritic traditions of written Hinduism, associated with the Aryans who invaded the north of the subcontinent in the second millennium BCE, and pushed the darker pre-Aryans further south, and also to the bottom of the social hierarchy. Although that pre-Aryan, non-literate culture is suppressed, you can see it in rural areas where there is music and dancing. Dalits are sometimes regarded as pariahs, yet this disapproving word has honourable associations in the South Indian language of Tamil from which it comes. There, the original pariahs were the drummers who announced the coming of kings. Dalits tend not to worship Hindu gods and goddesses, but instead turn to more primal images to focus transcendent presence in the world: so, in a sacred place, they might worship a tree and the mother goddess who personifies the earth. I was given a bronze statue of such a goddess. She is dressed much more simply and skimpily than in the saris of most Indian women. Her facial features are more characteristic of darker-skinned Dalits than of the usually, lighter-skinned caste Hindus.

I asked Professor Kenneth Wilson, of the Department of Philosophy at Osmania University, Hyderabad, for an exact definition of who are the Dalits, but he would not be precise. He said it could refer to anyone who is oppressed, though it is usually used of those who are, quite literally, outcastes. He pointed out that the constitution of India regards the Dalits as an economically disadvantaged Hindu group, below the four accepted castes. Yet this will not do. Most Dalits do not feel themselves to be Hindus, whatever Hindus want to believe.

It is not just small groups of Christians who have promoted justice for the oppressed. The great Dalit hero of pre-independence India was Dr Ambedkar, who chose to leave Hinduism and lead his followers into the Buddhist fold, where he hoped they would find more justice. This led Ambedkar into conflict with Mahatma Gandhi, the great icon of modern Hindu tolerance. Gandhi changed the name of the 'untouchables' into 'Harijans', literally, 'beloved of God'. Ambedkar thought this to be a piece of Hindu condescension, an agreeable name granted in default of any far-reaching social, economic and religious reformation that would really change the status of Dalits. Dr Wilson believed that Ambedkar had a point. He pointed out that Gandhi blocked Ambedkar's attempts to gain Dalits separate electorates in the political reforms of the 1930s, during the dying years of British India. He did so by threatening to fast to the death. However, these separate electorates were granted to Muslims, without Gandhi's intervention to prevent this. Nowadays, many Dalits feel that Gandhi betrayed their interests. Ambedkar is their abiding hero, but Gandhi almost a villain.

Some Protestant Christians have been at the forefront of working for social justice among the Dalits. The village in which Bishop Azariah grew up was a Dalit village; no one else lived there. He remembered what an impact was made in his life when, as a lad, he saw a caste-youngster refer to an elderly Dalit man as 'boy', and order him around insultingly. As he grew up, Bishop Azariah reflected from his Christian heritage upon this outrageous incident and its implications for so many of India's poorest and most oppressed people. His inspiration was the deliverance that Christ offers in Luke chapter 4 verse 16ff.: good news, freedom for prisoners, the recovery of sight for the blind, the release of the oppressed. The bishop said there is 'no nobody' in the dictionary of Christ; everybody is somebody. Dr Azariah has become a pioneer of Dalit theology, a Protestant theology of liberation for South Asia.

I interviewed many Jesuit priests, who were deeply impressive for being at the forefront of the struggle for justice in the subcontinent. Indeed, if I may obtrude my own opinion at this point, I would say that the Roman Church is, in many ways, the most vibrant of all ecclesial bodies in India, socially, liturgically, and theologically. Yet the Roman Catholic hierarchy is often socially more 'grand' and therefore more patronising than its Protestant and Orthodox counterparts, so priests doing splendid work on the ground do not always get the support they deserve from their superiors. One Roman Catholic Archbishop told me that there is no Dalit theology worth the name. He pointed to the fact that there are now some Dalits in seminaries, who are becoming priests. In his opinion, they should be grateful to be there. It would take time for these people to influence the system but, he told me, Rome wasn't built in a day.

As I played over the tapes of the interviews I made, certain questions formed in my mind, of which I was only rudimentarily aware when I did the interviews. The first major one was: for

Christians, will the Christian framing of a Dalit theology of liberation promote or subvert the Christian faith among the poor and oppressed of India? Bishop Azariah's own religious, economic and social status has been immeasurably advanced by his Christian commitment, and quite right too. Yet this is not true of most Christian Dalits, who remain poor and despised. The views of the Roman Catholic Archbishop are widely held, not just among Catholics but among many Christians from a caste background. As a result, although many Dalit laypeople to whom I spoke came from a Christian background, they obviously held not only Hinduism but also the Churches in considerable suspicion, sometimes even disdain, for their failure to improve the role of Dalits. Furthermore, the emphasis by some Dalit Christian interviewees upon the contemporary existence of what was originally a pre-Aryan primal faith could undermine Christian claims about the central importance of revelation through Christ.

This ancestral faith also depreciates any strong links with the written, Sanskritic traditions of Hinduism. A number of commentators sympathetic to Dalit aspirations, including Dr Eric Lott, a Methodist missionary who spent thirty years in India, latterly teaching in the United Theological College in Bangalore, sounded a warning about this. In his view, the Sanskritic traditions are simply too important to be dismissed or sidelined as oppressive and irrelevant. Rather, Dalits must come to terms with all the Indian historical past, and redeem it. The implication of much Dalit spirituality does, in fact, play down the claims of some Hindus and Christians. In the view of many Dalits, implicitly or explicitly held, the religious future for Dalits lies, not in any of the great world faiths, but in reclaiming their own spirituality, outside the boundaries of Hinduism, Christianity and other great systems of faith. Similarly, one could ask whether Hindu, Muslim and Buddhist Dalit academics (whom I did not interview, but who also exist) will manage to keep their focus group within the religion, or whether Dalit theology is not more likely to lead people back to an indigenous, aboriginal faith.

The second important question arising from my listening to the taped material was whether, in fact as opposed to religious mythology and imagination, there is a characteristic indigenous Dalit culture and spirituality. Maybe the hope of the 'oppressed ones' actually lies in a chimera, a flight of fancy. The parallel that came to mind was of Celtic Christianity, currently in fashion among some British Christians. Much so-called Celtic Spirituality has nothing to do with what the early British and Irish Churches were really like. It is, rather, the repository of the fantasies of contemporary middle-class churchgoers who are tired of the bureaucracy, pomposity, irrelevance and arid worship of much church life. As a result, they romanticise church life, belief and practice in their country's past and impose upon it their own hopes and dreams, rather than draw from that past what actually existed. In like fashion, a question mark needs to be put against Dalit spirituality. Clearly, there are millions of outcaste people in India, poor, and despised by others. Yet is Dalit religiosity actually an indigenous Indian theology? Rather, it may be an import from other parts of the world; a mixture of primal faith with its reverence for running water, stones, and local deities, combined with a Christian theology of liberation, derived from Latin America. One of the possibilities in the global village we now inhabit, with its interconnected communications, is that we can select bits taken from here, there and everywhere among the world's spiritualities, and mistakenly read them as an authentic expression of our own history.

I am not claiming that Dalit theology definitely is a hotchpotch of bogus beliefs and practices, still less that its ardent proponents are deliberately engaged in perpetrating a hoax, either on themselves or on others. I am suggesting that these practitioners could be mistaken in interpreting their past; there could be an element of romanticising ancient times in order to make the present bearable and the future hopeful. It could be that a Dalit religion will emerge that is quite clearly (at least to outsiders) an imaginative human construct, yet one which focuses the aspirations of many unjustly treated people for equity.

the question of truth

In the West, truth is often perceived as factual accuracy. So the myths of many religions get very short shrift from the secular-minded, who are short on imaginative visioning and empowerment. Elsewhere, truth is differently observed. In the West

Asian context in which the Christian Gospel of John was written, the author or editor used the expression of 'doing the truth' (John 3: 21). This implies, at a primary level, relationship with the Transcendent and a transformed life.

So, when members of Western religions look at other ways of believing or disbelieving, they often judge them by false criteria; other ones than a subject's relationship with ultimate reality, that changes her for the better. Rather too many Western religious and secular people are gripped by graceless and rather commonplace and confined certainties, inadequate and inappropriate for a plural world.

Broadly speaking, there are two attitudes towards the issue of religious truth, both of which are age-old and found in many if not all religions. I point to one such encounter between these divergent responses, from the late fourth century CE. The pagan Symmachus asserted that:

> The mighty secret of mysterious truth
> By many ways and different paths is sought.
> A hundred roads and varied ways must trace
> That course which searches out the hidden God.

The Christian champion, Ambrose, disputed these sentiments and resolutely responded:

> The truth is far from that: the following
> Of many paths holds only wandering doubts
> And straying more confused. Only the single way
> Avoids such error: no turning of the steps
> Into diverted ways, no hesitation
> Before a multitude of different paths.

The Buddha, almost one millennium before, came close to articulating a position similar to that of Ambrose, but that earlier contention was rather better nuanced: it provoked adherents of pluralism into asking, how can we *know* that there are many ways? To use a commonplace and rather over-used modern analogy: who has seen the top of that mountain which is the summit of all paths, and why was a vision granted her whilst the rest of us are left in swirling mist? If, rather, we hold to the view that there is only one correct path to the divine or from Transcendent reality to us, how can we know that *our* way alone is correct?

Sometimes, the two positions are, ironically, rather close, in the claims they make to a private, revealed knowledge. A Christian points to Jesus as the only way (by alluding to rather too free a translation of John 14:6) and a Vedanta Hindu believes that many and varied are the paths to truth. Both justify their different convictions by claiming that they are revealed to them by Transcendent reality. How can we know that our revealed truth is superior to another's?

So the terms of the controversy between Symmachus and Ambrose, which have resonated over many centuries, in different cultures and between different religions, may be inappropriately skewed. We need to share our deepest hopes and dreams in a form more suited to the diverse world in which we live. That very diversity may imply that Transcendent reality has not utterly set its face against variety and even innovation. This is not to maintain that all points of view are valid, but it is to claim that monolithic views of truth fly in the face of reality. To intrude my own view, as I get older I find that arrogant certainties convince me less and less: whether they are of the 'I am right, you are wrong' sort; or, indeed come in the guise of 'All of us are all right, but my superior tolerance makes me more right than you'. Some of my friends and acquaintances have been certain that their way of faith alone, whether generous or intolerant towards others, is correct; I have enjoyed their passionate commitment more than their indestructible certainties.

Yet, of course, people do set great store by what they believe and live by and, to that extent, prefer that way to different routes. Sometimes they explain their way to others. Often, they are prepared to risk many things, even life itself, not only to interpret their convictions about the ultimate mystery of living and dying but also to offer them to all who will hear and may convert.

Sometimes the life that they risk is their own; occasionally, it is that of the recipient of their wisdom. For example, in making one series of radio programmes on 'The Missionaries', I spoke to Suesanne Abraham, the Arabic Broadcast Ministry coordinator of the 'Back to God' hour, a radio ministry of the Reformed Church which broadcasts all over the world from just outside Chicago. She told me of people who write to her from North Africa and Arabia, telling her that they have converted to Christianity because of the radio ministry they have heard. Such people can be disowned, beaten up or even killed, by their neighbours or even by family members. Ms Abraham is mindful of the consequences of her work, and often encourages people to be secret Christians. But martyrdom has always been a Christian vocation for some, even today. They think it worth risking for the sake of the truth they have received. I know that such putting to death of members of one religion by another happens; in this case, by Muslims of Christians. I also know that many millions of Muslims are goodly and godly people. I have talked with many, and love some.

Not all people of faith are moderate. Indeed, 'moderation' seems rather a lukewarm word to describe a phenomenon like religion. Religion gives life but also deals death. A religious person with my temperament believes that he practises his faith when he talks with and interprets the faith of others; in my laid-back, courteous, questioning, rather 'English' style. Different people of faith die for what they believe, so some zealous people of faith would regard my work as the work of the devil or, more generously, as selling the pass. In their view, you should stand up for what you believe and defend it, not give a platform for others to spread their erroneous and vain opinions.

faith in the future of religion

If the view is true that religions enable Transcendence to dwell among humans, and that that end is of more importance than the various means of attaining it, then we would do well to listen to the voice of Wilfred Cantwell Smith, probably the greatest recent theologian of faith and religion. For Smith, faith is, in practice, more important than religion. He concentrates on 'cumulative tradition' and 'faith' as the two hinges upon which the door of historical religious development has swung (1978; chapters 6 and 7). Cumulative tradition comprises the communal dimension of religious life in which all its participants share. Faith is the process by which a religious person relates to the mystery of that which lies beyond her, to the 'divine' as it is differently named within the various traditions of faith. The meaning and end of religion is that humans should locate, through it, faith in Transcendent power, a transformative experience.

Can religion play a part in transforming people for good in the modern world? We can perhaps begin to answer this question by looking at one man who, though regarded with suspicion by many Dalits, was a symbol of hope for many more people in the twentieth century: Gandhi. Mohandas Karamchand Gandhi (1869–1948) became the *mahatma* or 'great soul' of modern Indian history. In 1893, before he became 'the spokesman for the conscience of mankind' (a tribute bestowed at his death by the then US Secretary of State), he was a young, London-trained lawyer, anxious to make a living. He arrived that year in South Africa to advise lawyers working on a big case for a firm in Porbandar, his hometown. A week after his arrival, he was travelling on a train from Durban to Pretoria, with a first class ticket. A white passenger objected to his presence. Asked to move out, he refused and so was ejected on to the platform at Maritzburg station on a freezing night.

This traumatic experience of racism fired his anger and sense of injustice. He stayed in South Africa for twenty-one years. There, he established all of the methods which he was to use in later life in India, to end discrimination and, eventually, foreign British rule in South Asia. He founded an 'ashram', the Phoenix settlement near to Durban. He developed his practice of non-violent resistance to perpetrators of oppressive laws, both businessmen and politicians. When he arrived in India in 1914, he was a hero, who had worked for justice for indentured Indian workers in South Africa. By the time of his assassination on 30 January 1948, he was god-like. The agnostic first Prime Minister of independent India, Jawarharlal Nehru, almost a son to the *mahatma*, broadcast on radio to the nation: 'The light that shone in this country was no ordinary light... it represented the living, the eternal truths, reminding us of the right path, drawing us from error, taking this ancient country to freedom.'

Gandhi called his version of non-violence, *Satyagraha*, which means 'truth force'. The impulse behind Gandhi's life was religious. It was a curious mélange of influences, including the Jain religion present in his native area, Tolstoy's works (Gandhi and Tolstoy exchanged letters in 1909), Quaker friends in London, his reading of the Sermon on the Mount and, above all, a very particular reading of the Bhagavad Gita. Fittingly, as he died, he called on the name of Ram, or God.

The consequences of such faith transformed the life of all Indians and many others. He greatly influenced Dr Martin Luther King, and Nelson Mandela, and through them, liberation movements for blacks in the USA and in South Africa in the middle and closing years of the twentieth century. Like him, their peace-making was inclusive, embracing opponents as well as allies in their intention to promote justice and human integrity. Like him, their activities arose out of strong religious faith. It is surely a sign of hope in the world we now live in that a Hindu, himself deeply influenced by Christianity and Jainism, should have become an exemplary figure for a Christian Baptist minister and a Christian Methodist lawyer. All three transformed the countries in which they lived.

Religion is too important and deep-rooted a phenomenon simply to wither away. Western scepticism is an eccentric view, a blip in human thought about what it means to be human. Most people have believed, and the majority still do, in living the mystery of life in reverence and hope.

The really important question for most people is not whether we should have religion but: what sort of religion should we have? I have intended to suggest throughout this book that it should open people up to an alluring Transcendent presence that is transformative for good and not for evil. Too often, to be sure, religion is destructive or else justifies the ruin and devastation of others in a parody of what it is intended to be. So religion can wreak or excuse destruction of the 'other' in Ireland, the Balkans, Sri Lanka and many other places. Yet it can also engender justice and hope, the things that make for peace.

If religion is to be a force for good in the global village of the new millennium, then it needs to be co-operative and not needlessly competitive. In other words, only when people belonging to different religions work together can they hope to release sufficient tolerance, compassion, grace and understanding by which individuals and societies can prosper and grow. Retreating into false fundamentalism or sentimental liberal romanticism will not do. A hard-headed dialogical process is the way forward, whereby people of differently-expressed faiths can encourage and learn from one another. An example of symbiotic influence between people of different faiths was given in the previous section, when we looked at the influence of Gandhi upon people such as King and Mandela. This process of learning from and inspiring people of a different faith is by no means a new phenomenon in the world's history. This theme is pursued in my book, *Inter-religious Dialogue: A Short Introduction*.

bibliography

Ahmed, A. *Postmodernism and Islam*. London, Routledge, 1992.

Ameer Ali, S. *A Critical Examination of the Life and Teachings of Mohammed*. London, Williams and Norgate, 1873.

Appleton, G. (ed.) *The Oxford Book of Prayer*. Oxford and New York, OUP, 1985.

Appleton, G. (ed.) *The Oxford Book of Prayers*. Oxford, OUP, 1988.

Aslan, A. *Religious Pluralism in Christian and Islamic Philosophy*. London, Curzon Press, 1998.

Assmann, J. *Moses the Monotheist: The Memory of Egypt in Western Monotheism*. Cambridge MA, Harvard University Press, 1998.

Barker, E. *New Religious Movements*. London, HMSO, 1989.

Bennett, C. *In Search of the Sacred. Anthropology and the Study of Religions*. London, Cassell, 1996.

Bennett, C. *In Search of Muhammad*. London, Cassell, 1998.

Bierce, A. *The Devil's Dictionary*. New York, Dover Publications, 1993 edn.

Bowker, J. *A Year to Live*. London, SPCK, 1991.

Bowker, J. *The Sense of God*. Oxford, Oneworld, 1995a.

Bowker, J. *Is God a Virus? Genes, Culture and Religion*. London, SPCK, 1995b.

Bowker, J. (ed.) *The Oxford Dictionary of World Religions*. Oxford, OUP, 1997.

Boyarin, D. *A Radical Jew: Paul and the Politics of Identity*. Berkeley, University of California Press, 1994.

Brandon, S.G.F. *The Judgment of the Dead*. New York, Charles Scribner's Sons, 1967.

Brown, J.M. *Gandhi: Prisoner of Hope*. New Haven and London, Yale University Press, 1989.

Burger, J. *The Gaia Atlas of First Peoples*. London, Gaia Books Ltd., 1990.

Bunyan, J. *Pilgrim's Progress*. New York, Signet Classic, 1965 edn.

Chaucer, G. *The Canterbury Tales*. London, W. H. Allen, 1949 edn.

Chaudhuri, N.C. *Scholar Extraordinary: The Life of Friedrich Max Müller*. London, Chatto & Windus, 1974.

Cohn-Sherbok, D. *Judaism and Other Faiths*. London, St Martin's Press, 1994.

Coward, H. *Pluralism: Challenge to World Religions*. Maryknoll, Orbis, 1985.

Coward, H. *Scripture in the World Religions: A Short Introduction*. Oxford, Oneworld, 2000.

Coward, H. (ed.) *Life after Death in World Religions*. Maryknoll, Orbis, 1997.

Darwin, C. *On the Origin of Species by Natural Selection*. London, John Murray, 1859.

de Beauvoir, S. *The Second Sex*. London, Jonathan Cape, 1953. (Eng. trans.)

Douglas, M. *Implicit Meanings*. London, Routledge, 1991 edn.

Durkheim, É. *The Elementary Forms of Religious Life*. London, Allen and Unwin, 1915. (Eng. trans.)

Eck, D. *Banaras City of Light*. London, Routledge, 1983.

Eck, D. *Darsan: Seeing the Divine in India*. Chambersburg PA, Anima, 1985.

Eliade, M. *Myths, Dreams and Mysteries*. London, Harvill Press, 1960.

Eliade, M. *Australian Religions,* Ithaca and London, Cornell University Press, 1973.

Farquhar. J.N. *The Crown of Hinduism*. London, OUP, 1913.

Ferguson, K. *The Fire in the Equations. Science, Religion and the Search for God*. London, Bantam Press, 1994.

Fisher, M.P. *Religion in the Twenty-first Century*. London, Routledge, 1999.

Forward, M. (ed.) *Ultimate Visions*. Oxford, Oneworld, 1995.

Forward, M. *Muhammad: A Short Biography*. Oxford, Oneworld, 1997.

Forward, M. *A Bag of Needments: Geoffrey Parrinder and the Study of Religion*. Berne, Peter Lang, 1998a.

Forward, M. *Jesus: A Short Biography*. Oxford, Oneworld, 1998b.

Forward, M. *The Failure of Islamic Modernism?* Berne, Peter Lang, 1999.

Foster, S. with Little, M. *The Book of the Vision Quest*. New York, Prentice Hall Press, 1988 revised edn.

Freud, S. *Totem and Taboo*. New York, Moffat, Yard, 1913.

Freud, S. *The Future of an Illusion*. London, Hogarth Press, 1927.

Freud, S. *New Introductory Lectures on Psycho-Analysis. London, Harmondsworth, 1973 edn.*

Freud, S. *Civilization and its Discontents*. London, The Hogarth Press, 1982 edn.

Gibbon, E. *The History of the Decline and Fall of the Roman Empire, vol. 1.* London, J.M. Dent and Son, 1910 edn.

Haddon, A.C. *History of Anthropology.* London and New York, The Knickerbocker Press, 1910 edn.

Harris, E. *What Buddhists Believe.* Oxford, Oneworld, 1998.

Hick, J. *The Rainbow of Faiths.* London, SCM, 1995.

Hill, J. *The Preacher and the Slave.* In *The Oxford Dictionary of Quotations,* 1980 edn., p.251.

Holm, J. with Bowker, J. (eds.) *Themes in Religious Studies: Sacred Place.* London, Pinter Publishers, 1994.

Holm, J. with Bowker, J. (eds.) *Themes in Religious Studies: Worship.* London, Pinter Publishers, 1994.

Holm, J. with Bowker, J. (eds.) *Themes in Religious Studies: Rites of Passage.* London, Pinter Publishers, 1994.

Holm, J. with Bowker, J. (eds.) *Themes in Religious Studies: Making Moral Decisions.* London, Pinter Publishers, 1994.

Holm, J. with Bowker, J. (eds.) *Themes in Religious Studies: Human Nature and Destiny.* London, Pinter Publishers, 1994.

Hooker, R. *What is Idolatry?* London, BCC, 1986.

Hornung, E. *Akhenaten and the Religion of Light.* Ithaca and London, Cornell University Press, 1999.

Huxley, A. *The Perennial Philosophy.* London, Chatto & Windus, 1946.

James, W. *The Varieties of Religious Experience.* New York, Longmans and Green, 1902.

Kant, I. *Critique of Pure Reason.* London, Macmillan, 1929 edn.

King, U. *Christian Mystics.* London, B.T. Batsford, 1998.

Klostermaier, K.K. *Hinduism: A Short Introduction.* Oxford, Oneworld, 2000.

Knott, K. *Hinduism. A Very Short Introduction.* Oxford, OUP, 1998.

Lott, E.J. *Vision, Tradition, Interpretation.* Berlin, Mouton de Gruyter, 1988.

Macintyre, A. *Marxism and Christianity.* Harmondsworth, Penguin, 1971.

Markham, I.S. (ed.) *A World Religions Reader.* Oxford, Blackwell, 1996.

Marx, K. *Critique of Hegel's Philosophy of Right.* Cambridge, CUP, 1970 edn.

Masuzawa, T. *In Search of Dreamtime: The Quest for the Origin of Religion.* Chicago & London, The University of Chicago Press, 1993.

McCutcheon, R.T. *Manufacturing Religion.* New York and Oxford, OUP, 1997.

Mehta, G. *Karma Cola. Marketing the Mystic East.* London, Fontana, 1981 edn.

Momen, M. *The Bahá'í Faith: A Short Introduction.* Oxford, Oneworld, 1999.

Momen, M. *The Phenomenon of Religion*. Oxford, Oneworld, 1999.

Morris, B. *Anthropological Studies of Religion. An Introductory Text*. Cambridge, CUP, 1987.

Müller, M. *Chips from a German Workshop*. London, Longmans and Green, 1867.

Müller, M. *Introduction to the Science of Religion*. London, Longmans, Green and Co., 1873.

Müller, M. *Lectures on the Origin and Growth of Religion*. London, Longmans and Green, 1878.

Müller, M. *Sacred Books of the East*. Oxford, Clarendon Press, 1879–94.

Müller, M. *Lecture on the Origin of Religion*. London, Longmans, Green and Co., 1882.

Nehru, J. *An Autobiography*. London, The Bodley Head, 1936.

Nehru, J. *The Discovery of India*. London, Meridian Books, 1956 edn.

Otto, R. *The Idea of the Holy*. London, OUP, 1923. (Eng. trans.)

Parrinder, E.G. *West African Religion*. London, Epworth, 1949.

Parrinder, G. *An Introduction to Asian Religions*. London, SPCK, 1957.

Parrinder, E.G. *Worship in the World's Religions*. London, Sheldon Press, 1974 edn.

Parrinder, E.G. *African Mythology*. Feltham, Newnes, 1982.

Parrinder, E.G. *A Dictionary of Religious and Spiritual Quotations*. London, Routledge, 1990.

Parrinder, E.G. *The Bhagavad Gita: A Verse Translation*. Oxford, Oneworld, 1996.

Parrinder, E.G. *Avatar and Incarnation*. Oxford, Oneworld, 1997 edn.

Quirke, S. *Ancient Egyptian Religion*. London, British Museum Press, 1992.

Rahman, F. *Islam*. Chicago, University of Chicago Press, 1979 edn.

Redford, D.B. *Akhenaten: The Heretic King*. New Jersey, Princeton University Press, 1987.

Robinson, N. *Islam: A Concise Introduction*. London, Curzon, 1999.

Schmidt, W. *The Origin and Growth of Religion*. London, Methuen, 1935. (Eng. trans.)

Sharpe, E.J. *Comparative Religion: A History*. London, Duckworth, 1975.

Shillington, V.G. (ed.) *Jesus and His Parables*. Edinburgh, T & T Clark, 1997.

Smart, N. *The World's Religions*. Cambridge, CUP, 1998.

Smith, D.H. *Chinese Religions*. London, Weidenfeld & Nicolson, 1968.

Smith, H. *The World's Religions*. San Francisco, HarperCollins, 1991.

Smith, M. *Rabi'a: The Life and Work of Rabi'a and other Women Mystics in Islam*. Oxford, Oneworld, 1994 edn.

Smith, W.C. *The Meaning and End of Religion*. London, SPCK, 1978 edn.

Spencer, H. *First Principles*. London, Longmans, Green & Co., 1862.

Spencer, H. *Social Statics*. New York, D. Appleton, 1865.

Twiss, S.B. and Grelle, B. (eds.) *Explorations in Global Ethics: Comparative Religious Ethics and Interreligious Dialogue*. Colorado and Oxford, Westview Press, 1998.

van Gennep, A. *Les rites de passage*. Chicago, University of Chicago Press, 1961. (Eng. trans.)

Ware, T. *The Orthodox Church*. Harmondsworth, Penguin, 1993.

Weatherhead, L.D. *The Christian Agnostic*. London, Hodder and Stoughton, 1965.

Werblowsky, Z. *The Meaning of Jerusalem to Jews, Christians and Muslims*. London, Colmore Press, 1988 edn.

Whaling, F. *Christian Theology and World Religions: A Global Approach*. London, Marshall, Morgan and Scott, 1986.

Whaling, F. (ed.) *Theory and Method in Religious Studies. Contemporary Approaches to the Study of Religion*. Berlin and New York, Mouton de Gruyter, 1995 edn.

Wiebe, D. *The Politics of Religious Studies*. New York, St Martin's Press, 1999.

index